Harry King

A Professional Thief's Journey

Harry King

A Professional Thief's Journey

Harry King
and
William J. Chambliss

MACMILLAN PUBLISHING COMPANY
New York

COLLIER MACMILLAN PUBLISHERS
London

Cover Illustration by Phil McKenna

Macmillan Publishing Company
866 Third Avenue, New York, New York 10022
Collier Macmillan Canada, Inc.

Library of Congress Cataloging in Publication Data:

King, Harry.
Harry King: a professional thief's journey.

(Wiley series in deviance and criminology)
Reprint. Originally published: New York: Harper &
Row, 1972. With new introd.
Includes Index.
1. King, Harry. 2. Thieves—Washington (State)—
Biography. I. Chambliss, William J. II. Title.
III. Series.

HV6248.K52A3   1983   364.1'62'0924   [B]   83-10579
ISBN 0-02-320710-8

Printed in the United States of America

Printing   6 7   Year   9 0

ISBN 0-02-320710-8

For
Truell,
Judy,
Lisa,
Lauren,
Lou
and
Tommy

The Emperor addressed him: "Why
art thou a robber on the main?"
To this the pirate made reply:
"Why dost thou so my trade disdain?
Because 'tis known I scour the brine
In a small narrow ship of war?
Had I an armament like thine,
I'd be like thee, an emperor."

Francois Villon

Preface

This work was originally published in 1972 under the title *Boxman: A Professional Thief's Journey*. The present edition is revised and the commentary updated. I am very grateful to Carol Luitjens for her encouragement on this project as well as Peter K. Manning, Michigan State University; Eleanor M. Miller, University of Wisconsin, Milwaukee; and Paul D. Steele, University of New Mexico who reviewed the manuscript for John Wiley. I also wish to thank colleagues and friends who, having used the book in their classes, encouraged me to write a second edition; especially important was Theo Maska. His enthusiasm, stemming in part from his discovery that Harry King's son was a student in one of his classes where the book was required reading, was invaluable. I am also forever grateful to my friend Harry King.

William J. Chambliss
Newark, Delaware
May, 1983

Contents

Introduction

The modern world is filled with occupations that are regarded as professions by those who hold them; these people proclaim themselves "professionals." To be "a professional" provides one with claims of legitimacy, status and income unavailable to the multitudes. Criminal occupations are no exception. Although not generally acknowledged, those closest to the action—the police, prison officials, and other criminals—recognize the difference between a professional thief and an amateur, between the sometimes burglar drug addict and the systematic check forger, between the hotheaded kid and the rational safecracker.

This book is about a truly professional thief: Harry King. He devoted his life to perfecting the arts, crafts and science of criminality. He succeeded in mastering his trade and making a living—"a damn good living" he would say—out of crime. As you read his story you may wonder if it was in fact a "good living." Whatever your judgment, Harry was satisfied that he did well with the opportunities offered him in the world he knew.

Harry was a professional thief from approximately 1910 to 1960. For the better part of those years he specialized in safecracking—in the parlance of thieves he was a "box man." This is his story. Through it we are provided a glimpse into a life-style, a philosophy and a pattern of living that is ordinarily obscured from our vision. By coming to grips with Harry's life we learn a great deal about America, law, crime and social relations.

I first met Harry King in 1963. He was fresh out of "the joint" where he had served a five-year sentence for burglary. On release from the penitentiary Harry decided he did not want to return to safecracking. Although he had spent a number of years in the penitentiary before, this had never deterred him from returning immediately to his criminal profession (in fact, as we will see, having spent time in the penitentiary actually increased his dependence on crime as a way of life). On release in the early 1960s, however, he decided he had had enough of "rooting and rousting about."

Why this change of heart took place is difficult to say. Harry had little respect for "square-john society." He saw the straight world as hypocritical and corrupt. Everyone, in Harry's view, was larcenous in their soul and in their deeds, especially those "respectable citizens" like judges, policemen and prison officials. The difference between himself and them or, more generally, between professional thieves and them, was that thieves were not hypocrites; they admitted their criminality and were willing to pay the price for it. Indeed, they took pride in it whereas the corrupt officials and business people of the world tried desperately to hide it.

At our first meetings Harry and I found it easy and enjoyable to swap stories and share a bottle of wine. At the time I was engaged in a study of organized crime and political corruption. My initial interest in talking to Harry, other than for the sheer enjoyment of hearing him tell fascinating stories and make insightful observations about the world, was to learn what he knew about organized crime. His knowledge of that subject was limited, however, while his life story was fascinating. I asked him if he would come to my class and talk informally to the students about professional crime. He agreed. The first few minutes of the presentation were pure agony for us both. Although Harry was normally articulate and talkative, in front of the class he was shy and reserved. I wondered for the first fifteen minutes if I could ever get him to answer anything with more than a "yes" or "no." But when I asked him if he minded spending time in prison his irrepressible sense of humor got the best of him:

> I didn't exactly like it. But it was one of the necessary things about the life I had chosen. Do you like to come here and teach this class? I bet if these students had their wishes they'd be somewhere else, maybe out stealing, instead of sitting in this dumpy room. But they do it because it gets them something else they want. The same with me. If I had to go to prison from time to time, well, that was the price you pay. On the other hand, I could buy new Cadillacs and $200 suits when I had found a fat mark. How often do you do that, doctor?

That opened the gate and the students were allowed a rare glimpse of a world normally closed to them.

As we spent more and more time together, I realized that Harry's perceptions and insights as well as his exceptional intelligence combined to give his story a quality often lacking in other autobiographies. I suggested to him that we work together on a book about his life. He agreed and we began in earnest.

I met with Harry at least twice a week for the next three years. I taped our conversations whenever possible. At first this made him nervous but after a couple of sessions he was comfortable with the recorder. When it was impossible to tape the conversations, I took extensive notes. When I left Seattle in 1967 I gave Harry a tape recorder and a supply of tapes. For the next year he regularly sent me tapes every week. I listened to them and would write or call him to discuss things on the tapes, points needing clarification or elaboration, or just to compliment him on a job well done. We talked often on the phone and I kept notes of those conversations as well.

In the end I possessed a pile of transcribed tapes, notes and observations that stretched from the floor to a foot above my desk. It was a massive array of disjointed material. The interviews were in reality only conversations and, like all conversations, jumped from subject to subject, time period to time period. I must have gone through the piles of papers hundreds of times searching for a way to tell Harry's story. I worked on it, on and off, for over five years and was not at all sure I could ever bring any kind of order out of the chaos.

One weekend Kai Erickson came to visit me in Santa Barbara where I was living at the time. I played a tape of Harry's for him. Kai was deeply moved by the tape and encouraged me to put the book together. In the middle of the night I awakened with a conception of how I might organize the materials. That outline became the chapters of the book. I also realized at that point that I should edit the work to give it coherence but let Harry tell his story in his own words.

Here, then, is Harry's story. It is a vital documentary of the life of a man—a man I grew to love and whose friendship I cherished. A man who suffered as we all do from inconsistencies and contradictions. A man who struggled against oppressive forces and who made his way in the face of obstacles and with an occasional flash of luck. A man who enjoyed parts of life, suffered from others and lived with dignity. A man who was a professional thief.

1

Becoming a Thief

I never could blame my life on my parents. I mean, I sit down and talk about it and say if it hadn't been for my mother I wouldn't have been a thief. I can't say that. But if you're built one way you're going to live that way—you know? There's nothing going to change it. It's just like why don't you go opening safes? I didn't know how to steal when I started, but I was inclined that way, or I wouldn't have done it. I have a brother who also became a criminal. I never had any contact with him until after he was a thief. But he did become a criminal and the other two didn't. My sister is a square-john girl. She knows that he and I are criminals. We don't know where my brother is. I think he might be dead.

I was born in Sioux City, Iowa. I went to third grade of school. I didn't like it, so I just quit. That's all there was to it. At this time I was ten or twelve years old and my mother and father broke up their family life and got a divorce. I had two brothers and a sister. I was the oldest. My mother had custody of us. It was impossible for her to work and take care of all of us. So she placed me in what was called a parental school. Of course, at that age, I didn't like being away from my home so I used to run away and go home. She would call the authorities and have them take me back because she couldn't keep me. I was very much upset because I couldn't understand why my brothers and sister could be home and I couldn't. At that time I had committed no crimes in any form.

It was while I was at this parental school that I learned that some of the kids had been committed there by the court for stealing bikes. They taught me how to steal and where to steal them and where to sell them. Incidentally, some of the "nicer people" were the ones who bought the bikes from the kids. They would dismantle the bike and use the parts: the wheels, chains, handle bars and so forth. Bikes were quite common in those days.

The majority of the kids were in there for crimes. They were so young that they couldn't be sent any place else. They were too young to go to the reform school. They were all under twelve years. I was there less than a year. I learned the names of legitimate dealers who would pay a dollar a piece for a bike, which is quite a large sum of money for a youngster. I was no problem child at that time but my mother had to do something with me since there were four children in the family. She had to have somebody take care of me and somebody had talked her into the idea of putting me there. She had to pay for me there.

After about a year my parents' divorce was settled and my mother took me home. By this time a wall had been built between my mother and me, after being at this parental school. I didn't have respect for my mother and my father was gone; I didn't know where he was. I felt that I had been rejected by my mother. My father was a railroad man. He was a conductor and a brakeman. My mother worked too. She had to try to keep the family together and at the same time try to support them.

I was wandering around one day, I happened to go up to the YMCA and there's racks of bicycles. All that day I never had it so good, I'll tell you, I was riding them away as fast as I could. Then we took them apart and peddled them. That was the start of it as near as I can recall. I was quite young then; in fact on about half of them bikes I was riding underneath the bar, not on top of it.

Then I just went from there on up. I ran around with a group of kids; I don't remember how large a group it was. Sometimes there would be a half dozen and sometimes there would be one. We would break into grocery stores and steal cigarettes and things like that. This went on for a long time. I wasn't going to school.

Then my mother and all of us moved to Aberdeen, Washington. But I just couldn't adjust to their family life because they had been close all this time. I felt that I was an outsider. I doubt if my mother felt that way. I ran away from home and went across the states. I think I was twelve then. I went all the way across the U.S. on freight trains. I went all by myself, I was kinda afraid to be with hobos. I celebrated my thirteenth birthday when I was in Chicago some place. Then I came back home.

I guess I had been cast by that time because I immediately got into trouble. It was real comical. I got into trouble because I have always had an insatiable curiosity about everything. I looked in the window of the post office one night. I climbed up on a garbage can. There was a safe open in there and it was full of stamps. So I just climbed in the window and walked over to the safe and took out a whole bunch of stamps. The next day I walked out on the main street—it was a small town—with a big bunch of stamps under my arm. I went from store to store selling them stamps at half price. Because of my age and because the post office was a little embarrassed about it—leaving the safe unattended and, in fact, I think they had all gone home—they charged me as a state juvenile. They sent me to Chehalis State Training School for boys. It was a federal case, but at that time the federals didn't have a reformatory. So I was turned over to the state and tried by the state.

Chehalis wasn't too bad if you kept your nose clean. The food was pretty good. I learned a great deal about crime from the other kids. One of the things we all dreaded there was punishment. They had two forms of punishment. One of them was to make a kid stand on the line at attention with the fingers on the seams of his trousers. They would make him stand there all day. That's pretty hard to do, especially for a young kid. The other form, they had a heavy piece of leather that was a half-inch thick and about four inches wide. They had drilled a couple of small holes in this. When they wanted to punish a kid bad, they would take him into this room and make him take down his pants and bend over a table. One of the officers would whip him with this strap. Everytime that they hit the kid the holes would make a blood blister. Then when they would hit him the next time, it would break that blood blister and make another one. I've seen some of those kids with pretty raw rear ends. These were young kids, not grown up people by any means. I don't know what the oldest one was there, but he was well under twenty-one.

I don't remember when I went in there and I don't remember how long I was there. It was over a year, I know. I don't recall the circumstances for granting my release from the institution. I don't remember if I was sent to someone or what. It's kind of hazy because its pretty far back.

Later I got into another beef and was sent to Monroe. It's a state reformatory. They called the other one a training school. I went to Monroe for a crime I don't even remember what it was about. I did two years there.

After I got out of Monroe I went to California. My dad was down there living in Oakland. He took care of me and tried to get me on the railroad, which I didn't want. I got involved with this kid and decided to steal a car. We decided to come up to Washington. We were arrested for this. I signed one confession and he signed another.

I went to San Quentin. They put me in the jute-mill down there, or at least they tried to. That's where they made burlap bags. I refused to work there so they sent me to Folsom, which is an exceptionally tough penitentiary. I did three years and four months up there. I was the youngest guy there; they had to keep me by myself all the time. I was still under twenty. While in Folsom I got to running around with a clique of thieves who had contacts all over. Then when I got out I was introduced to a guy who handled all the heroin in San Francisco: a guy named Black Tony.

In the Joint the clique knew if you were good or bad. If you were bad you definitely weren't in the clique. That's all there was to it. By the time you done any length of time, three of four years in there, why if there was any bad in you they would know it. They wouldn't reprimand you; they would just kick you out of their clique. If they thought you were worthwhile then when you were released they would tell you to go down to a certain pool room or bar and ask for a certain person. In the meantime they would send word down that you were coming.

They would give you some word to tell this guy so that he would know definitely that you were the right person. It usually pertained to some crime that the police weren't aware of. In those days thieves were very clannish, very close, and would help one another, more so than today. He would see to it that you were taken care of immediately, that you were harnessed up with a gang that was working or given a job someplace. I was given a job on the newspaper.

I was affiliated with a crew that was called the Hoodlums—the hoods. They lived south of Market Street in San Francisco. They were never allowed north of Market Street by the police department. If they were caught up there they were taken down to the station and interrogated. As long as they stayed around Mission and Howard the cops would leave them alone. Incidentally this newspaper that we worked for was south of Market Street.

I belonged to the Hoodlums. They wore Frisco jeans, double-breasted blue coats, and tailor-made caps. In those days a lot of guys wore caps. It used to befuddle us as to how the bulls could tell that we were hoods. All the hoods wore the same kind of clothing. We all went out to one place out in the Mission district and had our caps tailor-made and they were of very good quality. We paid a fair price for it. We would get up on O'Farrell, Geary or Powell Streets and the cops would pick us up. We couldn't understand why.

We all worked for the Narcotics Syndicate in San Francisco, which at that time was run by Black Tony. It was a pretty big operation even then. The Syndicate used to get its morphine from Germany and its opium from China. It came in through New York and was handled by the local narcotic wholesalers. Then it was shipped out to the West Coast. The morphine was bought in a can, an ounce can; it was called a piece. The most popular brand was the Rooster brand. It came in little tiny cube-shaped cubes of morphine. In those days they very seldom cut it [mixed it with any other substance]. They just divided it with a razor-blade into bindles and then sold it. There was a terrific profit to be made in it then.

Most of the guys who worked for Black Tony worked on a percentage. They bought the narcotics for a dollar and sold them for two dollars. In my case, because of my youth, I was kind of a mascot around there. I'd do anything. I had no fear of anything. I recall that one time a trunk load of morphine came into Oakland. At that time the depot for the trains was in Oakland. We would have to go from San Francisco to Oakland to meet someone or to pick up a trunk. They heard that there was some kind of heat on this trunk. So I said that I would go pick it up. They gave me the baggage check, which had been mailed to them from the East, and got me a small truck. I went over there and picked up the trunk because it really didn't bother me in those days. I put it in the truck and drove to the ferry and back to San Francisco. My orders were to drive out some street until I was overtaken and then turn it over to them. What they did was just tail me, which I didn't know until later on. There was so much money involved in this trunk full of narcotics that I had a tail all the time from when I left San Francisco until it got back. They followed me down the street until they made up their minds that I didn't have a tail from the cops. Then they pulled up alongside and stopped and took the trunk. I went back to Tony and it pleased him very much that I had gone and done that. Tony usually gave me money all the time, which was more than enough for me and my wants. I bought a car with it and things like that.

Besides dealing in narcotics, Tony's men were also pimps. There were quite a few girls who were using narcotics. Tony didn't control the whorehouses in San Francisco and he didn't indulge in it. But most of his henchmen were pimps. It was kind of a sideline with them. Several of them owned whorehouses in town.

Everything I did for Tony dealt with narcotics. I would take narcotics from one of his men—not him, for nobody dealt directly with him. My job was to pick the narcotics up from one of the wholesalers. There were several of them under Tony. I then delivered them to the retailers. We had a guy named Red, who worked for the paper, and he was a retailer. He was a wholesaler in a sense too. I don't know how you can define this. Let me say this. Tony received the narcotics from the East. Then he sold it through his dealers. He would sell it by the piece. It was still in a solid unit in little cubes. Then the dealers would cut it up into bindles and peddle it. I guess that in a sense that would make them retailers.

While I worked for Black Tony some guy put the finger on him. The guy who put the finger on Tony had been released from Folsom and was sent to Tony with a good name. Tony put him to work and the guy was arrested. He was so afraid of returning to Folsom that he made a statement that Tony didn't know about even with all his influence in the police department. So Tony got him sprung on this charge but it was too late. He had already made the statement and everything. The federal narcotic squads took it over and took it to court and indicted Black Tony. This guy who Tony had hired appeared as a witness against him.

Later on, the guy was found murdered in Los Angeles. Black Tony had a connection with the syndicate back East; I guess you call it the Mafia. I never became acquainted with them so I never have seen any of them. They are a mystical organization as far as I'm concerned. They may be real and they may not, I don't know. But I've never had any contact with them even in my trips back East. After Tony was arrested, it broke up the Narcotics Syndicate in San Francisco, which was a local syndicate.

After I left Tony I went to work for Red. He got me the job down at the newspaper. I rode around with Red and I carried papers. I gave, let's say, a hundred papers to each guy on a corner. I gave him twenty-five papers that had a bindle of narcotics in each one. They would be folded so that he knew which was which. I would just get out of the car and hand them to him without any fear. He would hold those papers under his arm with the papers that didn't have any bindles in them. Well if you came up to him and you were a hype [a drug user] and wanted to make a buy, he would give you one of the folded papers. I don't recall what the retail price was then. These guys supported their habit by peddling papers.

A guy named Hotslim Bang was the circulation manager of the paper. All the time I worked for the newspaper, I never got a paycheck. But every weekend I would go into the cashier window and Bang would be sitting there. He would look at me and then pick out a check, my salary for the week because I was on the payroll, and he would slide it out to me with a pen, face down. I would endorse it and he would take it back. I never did know how much money I was supposed to be getting. I was really paid by Red.

Quite a few of us did work for the paper. The reason for that was we had such good protection from the police department. The paper was the strongest paper in San Francisco at that time and they could square almost any beef. That was the reason we worked for nothing. We made our salary on the side. We stole or peddled narcotics, or something on that order, in order to make a living. Bang, for giving us the job, he got our paycheck. He cashed the check after we signed them. He wasn't involved in crime at the time, but he had been when he was young.

I can't recall how long I stayed in San Francisco after I got out of Folsom. I've been in San Francisco so many times to live that I've forgotten how long I was there. We did quite a bit of stealing while I was there. I was involved with crimes with Red. We committed a few burglaries together. One of them, I recall, was a fur store. The alarm was haywire and we found out about it. So we robbed the store.

I went from San Francisco to Portland, and it was there that I learned how to open safes. That's when I got acquainted with Denver Dick. He got his name from reading the Denver *Post* all the time. In those days the Denver *Post* daily was almost as thick as the Sunday edition of our own paper today. It had all the crime news in it and pretty near all the professional criminals subscribed to it. They would read about friends of theirs and people they had been associated with. Denver Dick was sort of addicted to the Denver *Post*.

I don't remember how I ended up with him. The same old thing of passing word around. I came up the coast and was staying with a couple of people in Portland. I met him in a bootleg joint one night. I liked him; he was an easygoing guy and everything and so I went on a caper with him one night and it worked real good. I took care of my end of the job so he asked me if I'd like to work with him. Some way or another he took a liking to me and he took me under his wing.

He was one of the last of the old time Pete men, as they were called. They used nitroglycerin. They used to travel by freight train from town to town. Most of them were users of narcotics in one form or another. Some were addicted to it and some weren't. Dick never was a hype, but he would take what they called joy pops. He could quit anytime he wanted or use it anytime he wanted. He travelled around the country and lived in third-class hotels. I don't know how much money he had. I've given it quite a bit of thought, and for the life of me I can't remember where he spent his money. He didn't gamble or nothing. He was too smart for that. He knew that gambling was a habit. He stole quite a bit. So he made quite a bit of money. He wore cheap clothes and lived in real cheap hotels. I suppose he spent it in bars and on narcotics. Very few thieves in the old days put money away. Modern day high-class criminals do. Their word was always good with the fix, the bondsmen or anybody like that. Which it is today. So they didn't need money at anytime for anything like that.

I worked for Dick for three years as an apprentice. My job was to go steal the dynamite and cook it up, which, incidentally, gives you a terrific headache if you smell its fumes while you're cooking it. I would steal the dynamite, take it out in the country and build a fire, get a can of water in it, cook it up and hide it away. We just used a very small amount of it.

I would also lay on the joints [places they were going to burglarize] that he picked out. It was my job to watch the joint for three or four nights and see when the door-shaker [night watchman] or the policeman would come by, what time they closed the place up, what time they opened in the morning and just generally watch what they did.

I did all the work and he was the brains. It was quite lucrative for me as I got an equal share of the loot. He was very fair and trustworthy as far as dividing it.

He had a very good reputation all over the U.S. He had friends all over and he introduced me to quite a few people. We worked, in fact, all over the U.S. together. Every town we went into, why he would know all the gangsters in that area.

Denver Dick was a past master at shooting a box. He could lift that door right off and sit it right where he wanted to. Or he could blow it clear across the lake.

I worked with him three years before he even let me shoot a box. Shooting a box is real touchy because the grease that you use in cooked out of dynamite and it's not the same consistency as nitroglycerin that you buy. Sometime it may be real strong and next time weak and there's no way to tell till you try it out.

Explosives today are not used at all on the West Coast by local criminals. Canadians use them a lot for some reason or other. They come down to Seattle and blow a box occasionally. I don't know where they derive their grease from. I haven't talked to any of them. But I have talked to police officials. They know that today most of the boxes that are blown are blown by Canadians.

While Denver Dick opened the safe I was on the point. I was a good point man because I tended strictly to business. Later I've had guys working for me and with me that were very poor point men. They played around and monkeyed around and they didn't tend to business. But with me it was a responsibility—a great responsibility because I was responsible for the other guy's liberty. So I tended to business very closely.

I eventually learned how to open boxes by talking to him. Then we would get what we called a cold caper where we didn't really need a point man, because the safe would be out of sight or something like that. He wanted me to learn so he would take me with him in there. I eventually learned all the different makes of safes. Some of them you could take a gut shot and open it up easy and other safes you couldn't. You could blow the door all to hell and it still wouldn't take on a gut shot. So you would have to use a jam shot. He taught me all about the different safes and how they operated. Mostly I learned in conversation.

In those days the safe men were very clannish. They hung out together most of the time when they weren't operating. You knew what area the other guys were at and things like that. They would talk about capers that were cold. They would discuss techniques of opening safes. If one guy discovered something new he would tell the other guys about it. It was a pretty close fraternity, much closer than it is today. I'm talking about what happened among professional criminals now—the guys that devote their whole life to crime, that's not just ordinary or normal criminals. We never let anybody become involved in our conversations that wasn't a professional criminal. It is a legitimate business to us. To us it is just as legitimate as it is to be a professor. We never gave it a thought. We took it for granted that it was legitimate. The only people we discussed it with were the policemen. All professional criminals consider it legitimate.

I just talked the other day to a guy who is on parole and has a cigar store downtown. He's a pimp along with it. He's a professional safe-cracker and I taught him years ago. He is very resentful toward the police department because they interfere with his business. He thinks that by all rights he is entitled to go out and open people's safes. He gets very unhappy about the fact that the police interfere with it. He voices his objections just like you read in the newspaper about people who object to the Vietnam war. He voices his objections to their objecting to his opening a safe. I don't think I've ever heard it discussed whether it was wrong. All you do is curse the police for interfering with it.

We [professional thieves] would never beat the average working man or anything like that—like for a coin or jewelry collection. During my career I was always proud of the fact that I wasn't a low-grade thief, that I didn't go in for sticking up these small grocery stores or opening a safe in one of them. I never stooped that low in crime. When I was a young kid learning, I stole anything. But later on I became a professional and started hanging around with professionals and learned from them that you didn't steal from a home or small place of business; you only stole from a big place that could afford the loss.

They didn't associate with small-time thieves, neither in an institution or out of one. In an institution small-time thieves are considered what they call dings. Professional criminals in an institution usually hang out in one part of the yard or other. They share one another's newspapers and magazines. They will do any favor they can for another professional. But if a ding or a small-time petty larceny thief walks up to them they will just sit there and watch him. They won't talk about anything. If there's somebody in our clique who is pugnacious he is likely to ask this ding, "What do you want here," and run him off. We never had anything to do with them because they were of no use to us. We didn't need them in our business, they weren't practical and they weren't capable so we never had any reason to become associated with them at any time.

I worked for Denver Dick for approximately three years. Then for some unknown reason, I can't recall why, he went away or I went away and we broke up. I then went on my own. Then a law was passed that made using nitroglycerin on a safe a forty-year prison term automatically. So everybody quit using it. There were only a few good grease men left anyway. The rest of the guys were pealing boxes all the time or burning them with torches. Later on burning took over.

After Denver Dick I never changed; I never found any reason to really change. Opening safes was just as lucrative as any of the rest and I never carried a gun 'cause I don't feel that it's my prerogative to take a life. I feel if you carry a gun, you better be ready to shoot it. Some donkey is liable to jump in your face with a gun in his hand, so you're going to have to shoot, and I never want to be faced with any such thing. I'd rather run. But some of the policemen that shot at me didn't think the same way about it, I guess. I got shot five times in my life.

I was rather progressive in my operations. I watched everything and picked up on methods. I found that a policeman would come along the street and I would be watching a joint, laying on it, and he would pick me up for investigation if I was sitting in the car by myself. Several times I would be swearing at some guy necking with a girl in a car because I was trying to case the joint and he was sitting there necking with this girl. It suddenly dawned on me, why not get a girl and sit in the car and neck with her everytime a policeman came by. So I acquired this girl, had her in mind previously; I was living with her. So she and I used to go out, and she was very enthusiastic about it. We would go out and lay on a joint. Everytime a policeman came by we would start necking. I could case the joint real easy. The policeman would never pay any attention to it.

One night I took this girl out and it was what we called a cold caper. The safe was in a back room. I had been bothered by this girl for quite a time; she always wanted me to let her open a box. Well I used to use her on the point quite a bit. She was very good at it. In fact she was too good at it. She quite often got suspicious of something that wasn't there. It was better to be that way then not.

This night I took her with me and I was going to punch this box. She insisted that I let her do it. So I knocked the column off and put the punch on the spindle and gave her the hammer and told her to go ahead and hit it. I held the flashlight on it. I never gave it a thought that a woman winds up like she's going to hit a ball with a scoop shovel. She took a swing at it and never ever hit the punch but hit me right on the hand and broke it. I had to go ahead and open the safe with one hand after that, while she sat in the corner and cried. She cried all night about that.

Other thieves would never use women. They didn't trust them. Only a few of them were married legitimately to a woman. Some of them were married, but they were married to whores, shoplifters, prostitutes. All of the thieves' women were thieves in one form or another.

One thief was married to some woman that had kids and a home and the other thieves couldn't understand that. A professional criminal can't understand how you can go home every night and be happy. They go to bed at five o'clock in the morning. They are out catting around or doing something, chasing girls, drinking, laying on a joint. They are very seldom true to one woman, very seldom.

The old pete men, like Denver Dick, never had a woman. When they wanted a woman they would just go out to a whorehouse and get one. But as far as having a girl, well that was a handicap to them. That's the last of the breed that used to ride on the freight trains so they weren't any place long enough to get involved.

I've never known of a girl safecracker and I've never known one to be used. When I used that girl I never discussed it with any other thieves because I knew that they would frown on it. They would ridicule me so I never discussed it with them at any time. They might ask me who I was working with, or something like that. I would say I was working by myself or I wasn't doing anything. Incidentally, this girl wasn't a prostitute. After her and I broke up she got married and the last I heard of her, she had three children in Portland. She was doing real well. She was no thief of any kind. She couldn't steal anything.

Women are positively fascinated by thieves. I found it very easy to pick up girls once they find out you are a thief. That's why thieves can acqure prostitutes so easy. Prostitutes are attracted by a thief. For one thing he is a provider and they like that. They will give him all their money just the same, but they like the idea that he is a provider. They don't want a square-john or a mark for a provider. They belong to the thiefdom. That's why if prostitution is allowed in a town, it will attract thieves. I've been in towns, especially in the East, where they allow no pimps to land at all but they allowed whorehouses. But here, in Portland and San Francisco, they allow the pimps to come in and right away your crime wave goes up.

Right now, all the guys I know, professional criminals, are pimps along with it. It's easier to have a whore; she's easy to handle. He can go away for a long time and he doesn't have to give her any explanation. She accepts the fact that he is going away. Of course he loses her occasionally. Someone else will move in on him. As a whole, they're easier to handle than square-john girls. A square-john girl demands attention, wants to know where you are going and why you were gone so long and things like that. A prostitute doesn't ask any questions.

This girl I was working with was a square-john girl. She had never been in any trouble. I don't recall how I met her but she knew that I was a thief when I met her. She was attracted to me, which I knew automatically. So we became close and I moved her in with me. We lived together and she took good care of the house. I no doubt had intentions of putting her to work as a prostitute. But prostitution isn't my forte so I guess I just let it drag along. I think that sometimes she worked as a waitress, I'm not sure. When I moved her in I was making good money so I just told her to quit work. Then I thought of using her to case these joints. I took all the money and just gave her what I wanted to. So I used her for a point girl after I spent hours teaching her what to watch for and things like that. The only difficulty was that a policeman might overlook a man walking down the street at night, but a girl walking down the street was almost for sure stopped and questioned. So I always had to be sure that she was placed in a position where she wouldn't be observed by the police.

At that time I used a buzzing system. I had a couple of batteries hooked up to the buzzer and a button and she would press that button. I never exposed her to the street. Occasionally, I put her in the car. She would lay down in the seat to where she could just barely look through the window. If it looked too rough, like I better be alerted, why she would honk the horn. I knew right away that there was something wrong.

Eventually this girl went back to Portland. Then I went down to Portland. That's when I became involved with the rackets down there. I knew these guys prior to Portland, but I was never involved with them before. I was with them for at least five years and possibly ten. I didn't do much safe work nor did I go to prison. I was involved with the law but that was because of what we were doing.

When I went to Portland I met Jim, who was running the rackets at that time. As near as I can recall, I met him through a mutual friend—a guy named Dixon, who was a con man operating under Jim's protection. He gave Jim a part of all his take. He was quite successful as a con man. He conned these old widows mostly. I had done time with Dixon somewhere, I don't recall where. He suggested that I meet Jim and talk to him. So I did.

I remember very plainly when it was. I was waiting on a corner and they drove up in a car. I got in and was very much impressed with Jim's eyes at the time. I never will forget them; they were blue and just like ice. No feeling or anything there. I found out later that he was that way too. Jim at that time was a pimp. He owned a whorehouse and three or four girls were working in it. That's about all he had. But he was well on his way because he had a marvellous personality and everybody liked him. He kept his word with everybody. All the thieves would come down to visit him, the high-class professional thieves. Then even at that early period he had a lot of connections with the police department. It was only at a later date that he went higher than the police department to the judges and things like that.

Jim got me a job working on slot machines for a guy named Emlou, who was the big man in Portland at the time. Later Jim took over the town from Emlou and then I worked for him.

Jim was a very heavy narcotic user. At one time, I stole narcotics out of drugstores and gave them to him. He paid me a weekly salary, which was a rather lucrative one. I don't recall what it was now but it was a good salary. I operated about three years on that basis. All by myself. I would go out and find a drugstore, rob it, give him all of the narcotics. The understanding was that I was to keep him in narcotics. So, sometimes I would have to work once a month and sometimes I would work once a week. It all depended upon the amount of narcotics I got out of a drugstore. I liked this operation very well. I can't remember what terminated it. I believe he made a connection where he bought narcotics. He was a morphine user. I got arrested or something, I just don't recall what it was.

Then I went to work as a slot mechanic for him. I worked in the shop and overhauled all the machines. I finally went to him and told him that I thought I should have a third interest in the business. He agreed because I was working long hours and doing a good job. I wasn't stealing any money from him or anything, like most of the mechanics were doing. As a third interest, I got a very large amount of money. As a matter of fact I never did know exactly how much I had coming. I know that there was a large amount of money in the safe at all times to my credit. It was rather a flexible deal. I never checked on it and I never asked. All I did, if I wanted money to buy a new car or make a trip, I would just go in the office and tell the girl that I wanted some money.

During that time I lived in a rather exlusive apartment house. Remember this is in the thirties. I paid $150 a month for an apartment. It was a beautiful apartment. I used to go home at night and read a paper and sleep on the couch all night, if I managed to get home. We had so much trouble with people robbing the slot machines that we were continuously busy with it.

I can remember when I would pay $250 for a suit of clothes and then overhaul a slot machine with them on and get them all greasy and take them off and throw them away. I didn't care. I wore the best clothes attainable. The only thing I was very conservative about was my cars. I never bought Cadillacs; I had no interest in them. I bought Fords and cars like that. I think I learned that from Jim; he never bought big cars. Fred, his brother, was a horse of a different color. He bought a new Cadillac every year.

Jim was well liked by all the thieves and his word was good. They could leave money with him or jewelry. He would take an interest out of it when he sold it. He was pretty fair with the guys so they always looked him up. We always had a mark or two for the guys that came to town so they could go take it if they were short of money.

During the time I worked with Jim I also got acquainted with a box man called Bad-Eye. From time to time Bad-Eye and I would go rooting. The majority of rooting with Bad-Eye was done in Oregon and Washington. We did make two or three trips that were quite far away. We went into Oklahoma once. But the majority of it was in Oregon and Washington. I use to suffer from migraine headaches which, incidently, I don't anymore. I don't know if quitting crime did it or not.

We broke into this drugstore to acquire the narcotics. One of my partners was a user. We acquired a large amount of dollys (methadone); they are a form of narcotics. We had these large jars full of them. One day my partner said that I should take a couple of them for my headache. So I went out to where we had this stuff planted and I took a handful of them and put them in my pocket and took them up to the motel where I was living. I laid them on the dresser just like they were legitimate. I took a couple of them and my golly they were really great. So pretty soon I was eating those things like they were popcorn. They sent for me to go down to Reno and help them with a score there. I went down there and I hadn't thought of taking any of those pills with me. I got down there and there was such a thing called the Asiatic flu right then. I told the guys that I just couldn't work because I have this Asiatic flu; I have to go back to Seattle and check into a hospital for a couple of days. This partner of mine came over later in the day and I started to tell him. He looked at me and asked me how long I had been using stuff. I told him that I had never used stuff in my life. He told me I was hooked, that he could tell just from looking at me. He said, you are sick, how long has it been since you had a fix? I told him that I never had anything. He started talking to me and he said that I was hooked on those dollys. I told him it couldn't be. He told me that I better go back to Portland and get some.

I started back to Portland and I had an awful time driving back, being sick the way I was. I got back to Portland and I still didn't believe him. I talked to this friend of mine who had been a hype for many, many years. I had given him a bottle of these dollys to give to his wife. She was having a great deal of trouble with her menopause. I met him in the restaurant about a mile from his house. I told him to call up the hospital and to make arrangements for me to have a room. He said alright. He said that there was no sense in my going to the hospital if we could treat this otherwise. He said he would go and get some pills to give to me and see how I would feel. I went to my motel and laid down. He handed me a couple of them and I took them. We sat there drinking coffee and in about fifteen minutes he asked me how I felt. I said that I felt fine and asked him what he gave me. He said, "I gave you some of those dollys and you are hooked."

You can believe that I got off real quick. I checked into the motel and stayed in bed for a week. I went out cold turkey, but I sweated it out. That was enough for me. I was so scared of it, that I might become an addict from it, that that was all I wanted from it.

While I worked for Jim I was arrested hundreds of times during this period but he was always able to fix it. But then I got too hot and not even Jim could get me off so I went to Salem for a five-year bit.

I did three years and four months, I believe, which was a five-year sentence in Salem. Having no money when I was released I immediately looked up a safe and opened it. I continued that for quite some time. Then I met this square-john girl and got married. I went to work tending bar. She was quite young but she was of age. I tried to settle down there but it was awfully hard. I was having an awful hard time of it. Consequently, I got myself in bad debts. The baby came and I had gotten all new furniture and appliances. I was so far in debt that it was pathetic. But I never had any true evaluation of money, and it meant nothing. I would just go down and buy whatever pleased her. If she wanted a new carpet on the floor I would order wall-to-wall carpet and that's all there was to it. The marriage went on the rocks mostly because of this. I became too upset, my check was too small. I worked at other jobs at the same time trying to compensate for it and I just couldn't do it. I insisted that she stay home since we had the baby. This was foolish; I should have let her go to work. It might have saved the marriage. Eventually she went to work and I didn't like it. It was the cause of the breakdown in the marriage. Her father and mother knew of my past and they didn't approve of it so that didn't help out any either. She went back to Portland with the baby.

I went down and borrowed $500 from a friend of mine because I was in no condition to work or do anything right then. He was a narcotic user and I knew it. To please him and to show my appreciation for giving me this $500 I went back to Seattle and broke into a drugstore to get narcotics to give him. But my mind was so confused that I wasn't thinking very clearly. I opened the safe and obtained the narcotics. I also got the money that was in the safe. There was a guy who was standing out in front of the drugstore waiting for the bus. I looked at the cash register and the drawer was closed. The indication is that if the drawer is closed the change for the next day's operation will be in the register. If the drawer is open, naturally it is empty. I reached up and pushed the no sale button. The man who was standing out in the front was a bar tender from around the corner. He had been ringing the cash register all night so it registered on his mind. He heard it through a window that was up high in the store. He knew that there was something wrong. So he went back into the tavern and called the police.

The police came and arrested me and I was taken down to jail and tried later. I was sent to Walla Walla for from one to fifteen years. When I went before the parole board they gave me five years. Seems like I'm always getting five years. I did most of this five years inside the walls and was eventually placed outside on the dairy farms. I immediately ran away and went down to Oregon. I heard that my wife was not taking good care of the baby. I was brought back and lost all of my good time for the escape. So I did the five years flat.

Upon my release I was placed on parole and sent to Seattle. I went to work tending bar for the same man that I had worked for previously. When I had done my parole I believe that I would have gone straight then if so many people hadn't tried so hard to help me. This is hard to explain. It seemed that every time I turned around they were trying to help me. Nothing could I do by myself. It was, "Harry open a bank account, you must have a bank account." I couldn't understand why I must have the bank account; I could go straight without a bank account just as easy as I could with one. So I opened a bank account to please them, but it didn't make sense to me. It was, "Harry do this, Harry do that; Harry don't associate with this kind, Harry don't associate with that kind." Nobody ever influenced me, I don't think. I think I influence other people but I don't believe there is anybody that has influenced me unless I wanted to be influenced.

When I was reaching the lowest point I got word from Portland that Jim was in serious trouble down there and needed help. So it was a good excuse for me to quit my job and go down to Portland to help him. What he needed more than anything was money. I can remember when he had lots of money and I could have any amount of it that I wanted. So the only thing for me to do was to go out and steal money so I could help him, which I did do.

I travelled all over the country during that time. But we always reverted back to Portland. I worked with a number of different partners. This was when we went East and stole from the syndicate too. But we always came back to Portland. We tore the town up. Moving around, as I know and every professional criminal knows, is the only way that you can lose the police. You can't settle down in any one place for any length of time or they will get your M.O., your method of operation, and soon have you under arrest. If you continue to move around all the time why it's pretty hard for them to catch up with you. I stayed in Portland too long and operated too long there. The result was that they eventually realized that it was me who was doing all the safe openings. So they just started concentrating on me. I can't cope with the whole police department no matter how smart I might think I am. It was only a mater of time until I was arrested. They had so many charges against me that if I live to a hundred years old I couldn't have done them all.

I had my attorney who was a fix in Portland and he managed to get most of the charges knocked off. He got me down to two charges. I had $100,000 bail in order to keep me from getting out. He couldn't get the judge to take that off or reduce it any. I ended up with two five-year sentences in Salem. I went to Salem and did three years and four months and my attorney cooked up a deal which was a flaw in the law that you could interpret two different ways. Read it one way and it said one thing and another person could read it another way and it would say another thing. He got the judge to interpret it our way and they brought me back to court. The judge took this second five years off my back and placed me on probation, which I came to Seattle and did.

That's when I decided I had enough stealing. Why I quit, I don't know. Nobody connected with me for any length of time, I'm sure, knows. I don't know why I went straight. I don't know myself to this day why I did it. Occasionally I think about it a little bit and I'm not quite sure if I did the right thing. But I don't think that way for very long so consequently I keep on going straight.

It was a good life at times. I never did envy anybody that was a member of society. Frankly, I haven't got a hell of a lot of use for society not when I been taking care of those members of your society— district attorneys and judges. I just don't dig this society, that's all. I can't help it, but I can't see it. I just got the wrong definition or something, someplace along the line pertaining toward it, but I believe that a man should be honest. Don't misunderstand me there but I just can't see it.

I'll tell you a little story: One time I go out and I'm real hot in the town—red hot—I'm a Catholic and I hadn't been to mass for quite some time and I don't think they got off my back long enough to let me go to mass even. But anyhow, I'm gonna take this joint and I go out there to get it that night, as hot as I am. I had a tough time with that box, and I didn't leave until five or six o'clock in the morning. Like all businessmen, I carried a briefcase to carry that money in. I go out and get in the car and I just happen to glance in the mirror and I see this prowl car pull out about two blocks down the street. I said, "Oh, Oh," and they started after me.

Well, I ain't worried about them too much if they stay as an individual, which quite often they do; they want to be big heroes, so they don't call into the station askin' for help. They had my license number all the time. They always got my license number. And I started down the street and I'm thinking, Let me see, what'll I do, which way'll I go? I was thinking seriously of pulling in some guy's garage and just closing the door, hopin' the guy don't show up. And I went by this church, Catholic church, and I said, "Handy, I'll go to mass." So I sneaked in behind some cars and went on in the church. And while I'm in there I happened to look across and there's the district attorney I just got through fixing a short time before. He's very pious.

What brought this story to my mind is that this morning I went to mass and there's the judge that I've done business with two or three times; he's in there lookin' very pious this morning and I watched him for a while. That's why I don't have a lot of respect for society. When they go to church on Sunday and the rest of the week they got their hand out all the time, not all of them but quite of few of them and I unfortunately have come in contact with all that type. So it's got me just a little soured. I've met some real wonderful people since I started to go straight, though, I'll tell you. But I just can't accept this society. My parole officer beats on my head and the judge beats on my head: "You are a member of society now." And I don't feel any different about it than I ever did. I don't know.

2

The Mark

*"Every other joint pretty near is a mark. . . .
You find marks everywhere."*

I'd count what I had in my pocket. If it was necessary to go to work, I'd go to work. I'd just go out and get a score, 'cause there is a million of them. I walked up and down any district in any city and I see so many scores. Every other joint pretty near is a mark and some of them are good marks, too. You have no trouble gettin' a score. You find marks everywhere.

Sometimes guys will come and tell you about a score, for a percentage of course. Square-john guys—legitimate members of your society. A number of years ago a guy came and told my partner that when the kids register at the University there is a lot of money in the safes. So we went out and looked the place over. They had a couple of safes there and when we went out they had wired the place, bugged it. They spent quite a bit of money wiring it up, putting in a burglar alarm. But you could get around it real easy.

We stood there at registration with all the kids registering. I don't know what I would have said if somebody had asked me what I wanted or if they could help me. But nobody did. We figured it was a real easy mark. We could have taken it easy but we got distracted and took some others instead.

There are guys who make a good living finding marks for thieves—they call him the finger-man. These are people who live in the town all the time—legitimate people. Then when the crews of safe men come into town he'll give them two or three marks and they'll go look them over and if they like one of them, they'll take it and he gets ten percent. I know guys who've been operating like this for years. Everybody thinks they are members of society; your society, not mine.

I usually don't accept capers from a finger-man. I go find my own because there are so many of 'em. Because I have enough to worry about; the caper, plus the box, and getting it organized. I have enough to contend with without worrying about the person who gave this to me. Maybe the pressure's been put on him by the police department to set me up. They'll tell him, "Well, we've got you for this or that; now you set this guy up and we'll let you go." If I trust the guy, I go ahead and take the caper from him and he tells me that on a certain night the dough will be there. I accept his word and I go on the caper and, bang, I've got a rank. So I don't accept it and if a businessman or professional man came to me and tried to talk me into something like that I would have nothing to do with it because I would be wary of a trap.

It's hard to tell how you pick the mark. It's a thing you just do automatically. Thieves predominate in certain bars; like here in Seattle if I wanted to find a guy I'd go to two, three bars here or hotels where they'd live. I'd just leave word; I wouldn't ask for him. I'd let him contact me, that's his prerogative. If I want a score I just ask him, "Have you got anything going here?" If he has, then he'll give it to me. They do that. I think it's just a form of code; they just do it just as I would even today for friends of mine that I know are rootin'; if they came in town asking if I know of a mark, I'd say, "Yeah," if I knew where there was one and tell them where it was at. 'Cause that's their decision to decide whether they'd want to do it or not.

When you think you've found a mark, you just have to lay on it; you have to figure out the amount of business the store is doing. If it's a supermarket, the number of cashiers that's working, and you check it to see how often they are working. You can just about tell how much take there is by the number of people goin' in there and you tell how much money is in there. And you watch for the money wagon (the pie wagon we call it) to pick it up. If they don't pick it up it's going in the box that night. Then you pick the best day and you lay on it for two or three nights to make sure the doorshaker (night watchman) can't get in—hasn't got a key, which most supermarkets don't let them have. But you just watch the place when he shakes the joint down and the night when you've decided to root then you go and root.

You might lay on a mark for months but the average supermarket, you're almost safe if you are real short to go right into town and hit it. That's all there is to it. I mean, they are all the same. Talk about criminals having a method of operation; so do square-johns. You stop and think, why you do the same things day after day, almost; you follow a pattern. It's the same way there; you're almost safe to go on in and lay on it till two, three o'clock in the morning and see how the bulls hit it and go ahead and work. It only takes you about half hour to hit one of them round-doors [round-door safes] if you don't run into any trouble. You always take a point man with you to keep watch. He can work inside or outside. We don't like to have him inside and if you're using radio, well, you put him on the roof as a rule, either across the street or right on the building. You try not to put him on the building because that draws somebody's attention. There is always some hoosier that's up at that time in the morning lookin' out the window. And you try to put him in some position where he can cover the area if you're usin' radio, and if you're not, why, you'll put him right out in front of the building.

It all depends on what area it is as to how you dress him. You dress him like the people in the area are dressed. Put him down in industrial areas you put coveralls on, give him a lunch bucket, and he can stand there all night and them bulls wouldn't even look at him. They will go right on by him. I don't have too much respect for some of their abilities, really. A lot of it I have, but some of it I haven't. If there is no place for him to stand outside, I put him inside. Let him look out. Well, that don't give him very good coverage like the back door or something like that, and if I have confidence in him I pay no more attention to him.

Being a point man is a job that's complete in itself. Of course, the point man usually does the casing for us, too, because the box man himself is usually too hot. They're more afraid of a safe man than they are of anybody else. There is more chance of identifying a man who sticks up the place. They just go down and get so many mugs, take them out there and chances are he'll be identified among those pictures. But a safe man, he comes in the middle of the night and leaves in the middle of the night; nobody sees him. So it's harder to identify him, and the bulls dislike safe men more, as a rule, so we usually use a point man.

I walked into a Safeway in Portland one night and gave the girl a $10 bill. She tried to give me change for five. I became very indignant and I leaned over to show her that there was a mark on this bill. By accident while I was standing waiting to hand it to her I noticed this mark. I leaned over and there's my picture on the cash register. I wasn't aiming to pay any attention to the place, but they'll do that with a safe man. I was tearing Portland open at that time and they knew it and they just couldn't catch me. They were trying to find out where I was casing the place and that's where I use a point man; he usually isn't hot. The guy that opens the safes is usually hot. And he's the guy they want, and I was the guy they wanted. And eventually, I'm the guy they got.

If I went to an Eastern state, I'd beat the syndicate. Have no misunderstanding. I beat the syndicate's joints. They got a joint and the thieves there are afraid to do it because they'll cool 'em off [kill them] if they catch them. I used to think it was a big joke to beat a syndicate joint, you know. There is a town—Covington, Kentucky—that was wide open. A girl I used to know was a hustlin' girl, you know, and I used to know her before she ever turned out. She was a youngster— so to speak—about seventeen–eighteen. And she went back and she was turned into a dealer—a twenty-one dealer—and she was a cheater, you know, a real good cheater. So she went back and went to work at Covington, right across the bridge from Cincinnati. She came out here to visit her mother and she was telling me about these two or three marks. The gambling joints had a big chunk of dough in them. So I said, "Let's go get 'em." But she said, "But they're syndicated joints, Harry."

She said a guy came out from the syndicate in Cincinnati and would make the pick-up once a week. But she knew what day it was and everything. So I told her to just go and get keys to them joints. So she went to work and through hocus-pocus she got hold of the key to the door and got an imprint and sent it out to me and I had a locksmith make it up. A crooked locksmith would make it up into a key for me and send it back to her and let her try it. When the time came I went back there and got three out of the four joints. And I thought it was a big joke—it never did come out in the papers, you know, naturally, but that syndicate went crazy.

I guess they tore half of the hoods up in Cincinnati trying to find out who did it. We did it from out here. Cause we had no fear, no respect for the syndicates—heck with them, you know. But they keep them guys pretty much in line back there. Because they cool them off real easy; they don't care. Life means too little—guys at the head of that syndicate, you must remember, were raised in the same area as these kids are that work under them; only they're smarter so they run the syndicate.

It's the same as anything else; one guy's the boss just because he's the smartest. Well, that's the same way with them. Don't underestimate people like Lucky Luciano—those people were smart; they weren't just pimps. Don't belittle them because they were pimps.

They were pimps in this respect, that they owned the higher whore-houses, not just one girl.

Talking about traveling around the country reminds me of one experience. One time we pulled into this town late at night that we were going through. I saw this general mercantile store. I told my partner that all the money in the town was in that store because there was no bank there. That's the way it usually is. We went all around the building and looked at it. We couldn't see any signs of anybody living there. I banged on the back door and nothing happened. No lights came on or nothing. I told him we should just go right in the front door. We figured we could jimmy it open and then jimmy it back shut after we got in. It was a double glass door. It had panes of glass in it. I was trying to get the jimmy in so it wouldn't make any marks on the wood. I was trying to work this jimmy in and I happened to look at something. There was a light inside. Here was a guy standing there in his nightshirt with a pistol in his hand. He was just standing there looking. I just pulled the jimmy back out and we walked away. The guy just stood there and looked. He never raised his pistol or nothing. We drove out of the town and went on about our business.

I found that up in the northeastern part of the state that it was hard to find money. They are so tight that they won't even buy a safe. They hide their money. We broke into several places up there and no safe. We got to checking around and talked to thieves in that part of the country. You have to learn to find where they have hidden the money.

The best place to find safes in homes was in California. It has a terrific amount of wealthy homes. Every one of them has a safe that is built into the wall. All you had to do was cut the plaster loose from it and pull it out of the wall. You have to be careful when you haul it off because if you drop it on the pavement it will probably come open. These people put a lot of money in there, a lot of jewelry, stocks and bonds. They were outrageous safes. All you had to do was hit them a good one and they would come open. If nobody was home we would get them right in the house. They usually have it in the study or something. They think it is real fancy. They put it behind a picture or something. All you had to do was walk around the study and pull up the pictures and look. Some of these safes you can actually open with a can opener. We call them cabinets. They are actually made out of tin and you could take a can opener and punch a hole in it.

With a box man the amount you find in a safe can vary any place. Today they're sending money over in these pie wagons—Brink's armored cars—every day and guys are lucky if they get $5,000 out of a supermarket. When we were working, we'd get $15,000–$20,000 out of one of them with ease. You know, I mean if we didn't, we thought we were beat.

One time we laid on a supermarket. It had a cabinet in it. We knew that we could open it in nothing flat. We had to go through the skylight to get in there. I took one guy with me on this job. It was in the middle of winter and it was extremely cold. We couldn't see the safe from the street. You could only see it from the inside of the store. He opened the back door after we got in through the skylight because I was holding the tools. The tools are pretty heavy. I opened up the safe and there was nothing in there except a couple of pieces of paper. I pulled them out and looked at them. They were copies of deposit slips and about a year old. Bank deposit slips. I turned my flashlight in there and I could see dust all over the safe. I told my partner that there was something radically wrong. We finally came to the conclusion that they didn't use the safe anymore and that the money was someplace else. Well to look in a supermarket for money is an impossibility. Everyone has a different conception of where they want to keep their money. We didn't even bother to look. The next day an article came out in the paper about it. Well this guy had bought this supermarket about a year before and in the transaction he forgot to get the combination of the safe. In the meantime he was hiding the money someplace in the store. He just got in the habit of hiding it and letting it go at that.

You can never tell what you are going to find; it is always a surprise. Sometimes you just have a mediocre mark, just enough to get an apartment or whatever you decide to get—a motel—to let you get established there.

I spent around $4,000 on a big dairy in Oregon one time. It doesn't matter; it's so many years ago down in Medford. We laid on this place and laid on it. Kept going down there, and down there, and when we finally got it, there was just one penny lying in the shelf in the safe. I guess they must have overlooked that penny. I was so mad I took it. So it's hard to tell. The supermarkets up until the last four years average $15,000–$20,000. That's fair size supermarkets: Safeway, like that; Lucky's, in California. California has the best supermarkets; Oregon is next.

We would find our marks by taking what we call road trips. Somebody calls you up from Los Angeles and you call up your partner;

maybe he's got some dough, you know; maybe he's got a new girl or something and he don't want to go. So you have to hunt somebody else. And sometimes the guy who called you has put a little clause in it, that you have to take somebody from down in that locality with you. But usually you work three or four years with the same partner. If the guy who finds a mark is another thief I usually take him with me or something like that. But it would depend on who it was. If it was one of my partners and he didn't want to work, he would just give it to me. A guy just called me the other day, about a month ago, and asked me if I wanted to go over to Butte—there was a real good mark over there. He asked me if I'd go over with him and take it. He was just doing me a favor because you're always doing them favors. I told him I didn't want to go so he and another guy went and got a good score, over $30,000.

3

The Caper

"It's a challenge, the whole operation. . . ."

When I'm ready to go out and get a safe, it's like I have a metronome inside my head. The minute I start to get ready to go out and root I keep this image of the metronome clicking back and forth at a steady speed. If it stops clicking that way, then I back off and wait for another night when things will be just right. I don't have to see anything. It's a sixth sense thieves develop.

When you steal, you're working against terrific odds. One little slip will make a great deal of difference. It's just like shoes. One time you normally wear an 8 shoe and you wear a 10 shoe and the next time you wear a 6 shoe and cut the toes out of them, just to throw them off. It gives you a sense of satisfaction.

It's a challenge to go on a caper and I spend a great deal of time afterwards going back over a caper and checking out where we had made a mistake and trying to analyze why I made the mistake—where I went to sleep on it.

When you go out, you're under such a tension by the time you go to root that I'm always nervous. Right up to the time I walk in the door. The minute I make the entry, then I'm in my field. I mean everything begins to bang-bang right down the line. That's the way it should be, but until you make the entry anything can happen. Some donkey's walkin' his dog or something just as you start to go in the joint, or some prowl car decides to double-back or somethin' like that. So you're under terrific tension, right up to the minute you go to work. The minute you go to work opening the box you're all right. From then on it's just normal.

Every box is a tough box. If a box has been rebuilt, why then they make it tougher. Some people, though, buy some of the most simple simons in the world, trying to convince the public that it's a good box when it isn't.

You take the box itself as part of your work, which is even still quite a challenge to me. When something starts to go wrong on it and if it isn't falling in place the way it should then I wonder why. I sit right in front of a safe and smoke a half a packet of cigarettes sometimes trying to think what's wrong here.

When I first started opening safes we used grease, nitroglycerin that we cooked ourselves. In using grease you only use two or three different shots. There is the jam shot, which is around the edge. You soap up the crack and make a cup on the top and pour your nitroglycerin in this little cup. It will run down this crack and around the door. The gut shot is when you take the combination, you knock the column off, you make a cup there, and you pour the nitroglycerin into this cup and it runs into the combination. When you take a gut shot you can stand right there and hold onto the handle and put pressure on it and pull on it. When the shot goes off you can't get hurt. But in the jam shot it will peel the whole door. So you should take something to put in front of it. A rug or mattress.

The gut shot is right directly into the gut box and it blows the tumblers away so you can just turn the handle. You can take a stick and then a rubber band on the other end of the stick (a large rubber band from an inner tube) and run it over to the hinge. That puts pressure on the mit [handle]. When the shot goes off that will automatically turn the handle. I saw Dick sometimes just stand around the corner from the box and just hold onto the handle and when the shot went off he would turn the handle right away. Because occasionally when you take a gut shot it would release the bolt for a minute and then would jam it again. It would force the disc into the bar and jam it so it couldn't be opened. Then you would have to take another shot at it. So it's advisable to have pressure on the disc so that you could catch it just as it went off.

The guys apprenticed under Denver Dick were very good at what they called a keister. It's a small safe inside of a big one. It has thick walls on it and it's very hard to give. He was very capable of blowing a keister. There are three or four different-sized keister. A quarter, half keister that runs across the top and a full keister that takes up half of the safe. Jewelers use them and things like that. They used to be good money chests. One thing, when you blew them then you would bend up all the silver that was in there and burn the money. The flash back would burn the money. That's one of the first things the police look for when a safe has been burnt with a torch or blown. They circulate the word around to banks to watch for money that has been burnt on the edges.

We don't use grease any more—now we punch or peel a safe but we never use grease. And we don't listen for the tumblers to tell us the combination like they do on TV: that's a lot of bull.

But before you get into the safe you have to get into the building. The fact is that every building has four walls and a roof and a floor in it and any one of them is a means of entry. Any one of 'em. You have to find a different means of entry in every one of 'em. I learned this many, many years ago when I was a youngster. A smart detective, see, he tipped me off. I had a habit of working Sunday evening and that way I got Saturday and Sunday's take out of these supermarkets and I would work exclusively on Sunday night. One night they pinched me on the street, just roustin' me, we call it; they gave me a bad time. They took me down and I just laughed at 'em 'cause I knew that they didn't have anything on me. This bull told me, "You think we don't know you're working only on Sunday?" I changed that right now, you can believe it. So after that I've changed and every caper, I try to approach it in a different manner, and it's a challenge, believe me, to think of another way because you find a transom or a skylight or a door or wall that's simple and you want to revert to it automatically.

When I find one means of entry I'll use it three or four times, then I'll go hunt a couple of guys I know and tell them about it. Then I change. They automatically go right out right now and start using it and they wind up getting caught probably. 'Cause the bulls are all watching for that means of entry.

It's a challenge, the whole operation, especially when you're working with a couple of guys because you have to watch them all the time irregardless how good they are. One guy, one night I've got him on the point inside the store. It was snowing outside and I brought him inside the store and put him in the front window and left him there and pretty soon I had to stop. I was working on a real tough box, and I had to stop and rest for a while. I thought I'd go have a cigarette and see how my partner's doing. I went up in front and he ain't there. So I think right away, "Where can he go?" So I went over and the son-of-a-bitch is eatin' bananas. And he was considered a very reliable point man, but he just decided he wanted some bananas. He saw them hanging over there and he went over and got bananas. I guess he decided he'd worry about the point later on.

So part of your job is to keep them guys in line, you know, and watch them closely and all the time you're working on the box, you have to think of that; when you lay out the caper you have to simplify it for them. You can't get it complicated or they get all mixed up on it; they're supposed to be goin' out one door and they'll go out another one. They'll probably collide and the bull'll just pick 'em both up, things like that. You have to watch real close, even your partner when you work. Not only that but they want to go right downtown that night and spend all the money, which is taboo.

One thing that I have found is that professional criminals who don't drink to excess or who don't use narcotics have a sense of disaster. They are like a wild animal. They sense and feel things before they actually happen. One time I was opening a safe that was sitting in an island in the front of the store. It was out of sight from the streets. But in order to open it you had to stand up. Over in one corner of the store was a little place you could stand in without being observed from the street. This street corner was a transfer place for the bus so there were always a great many people around there at all hours of the night. I took my partner and put him over there in the corner. I went over and started opening the safe. I had a great deal of trouble with this rebuilt box. Every locksmith has his own conception of what a burgler-proof safe should be: usually by adding more iron, which is merely an inconvenience because you are going to get the box open anyhow. I was having trouble with this safe. All of a sudden I sensed that something was wrong. I knelt down and waited and didn't hear any noise. I looked up and over on the edge of the counter was my partner leaning over the counter watching me open the safe. He was supposed to be clear over in the corner on the point.

Usually when I'm stealing I have a warehouse. Safecracking tools and safes that I want to experiment with are there. We have stolen two or three trucks and have put them in the warehouse and have left them there until they cool off. Then if the occasion comes up that we need one to kidnap a box we have it available. That way we don't have to use a hot truck that they might be looking for.

When I was with Bad-Eye we had a warehouse. We bought what we called the sedan delivery trucks. We had two signs made for the trucks. One was for a plumbing company and the other for an electric company. We had an understanding that at no time would we use these trucks except on a caper. We never took them out of this little warehouse that we had. We had all our tools there. Whenever we bought hammers, bars, etc., we would buy a whole bunch at once. We would keep these signs stored inside the trucks. When we went on a trip we would take that sign off and put the other one on. That would throw the cops off. During the year we would steal license plates and put them in storage so they cooled off. By the time we were ready to use them they were off the hot list.

The last time I was arrested I had a warehouse that had a great many tools in it: electric drills, saws that I was experimenting with. After every caper I took a certain percentage off the top, put it in the kitty. That was my money for experimentation. My partners were glad to have me do this because they had no interest in progressing. They were perfectly satisfied just to follow along with me. There were several metal cutting saws on the market and I was experimenting with them. We had also kidnapped several boxes that were unnecessary to kidnap. I could have opened them right on the caper, but I wanted to experiment with them. So we would take them down to the warehouse and I would take the back out of them. That way I wouldn't damage the door. I would reach in from the back and open the safe. That way I would have a whole door to work on that hadn't been defaced in any way.

At the time of my arrest I had a dozen safes in there. There was quite a commotion when they found out where the warehouse was. When my picture appeared in the paper, the woman who lived in the same block that the warehouse was in recognized my picture and called the police. She told them that she had seen me in that vicinity and so they went out and investigated. They checked around until they found the warehouse.

To me stealing was a legitimate business. It had a high operational cost, very risky and things like that.

One time we broke into a hospital where the drug room was. I usually wear coveralls. I discard them and my socks and so forth because they could be impregnated with concrete or metal from the safe and they could check back on it. The FBI is very capable of that. I find it much easier to invest a few dollars and my shoes and overalls and throw them away as soon as the caper is over. We went out to this hospital and the drug room was in an annex away from the wards and patients. This box was filled with narcotics. We opened the safe and found that they also kept the money in there. We didn't expect that, it was kind of unusual. I told my partner that I would take this box out while he filled the other one up and then I would come back and get the tools. I had just started down the corridor and the nurse came. She asked me if I was the maintenance man and I said yes I was. She asked me to come up and fix something. I said I would as soon as I took the box out. I often wonder what she thought the next morning when they found out that the drug room had been robbed. I'll make a bet that she never told anyone that she had seen me the night before.

One night we broke into a nightclub. It was up on the second floor and we cut down through the roof. We had never been able to see the box in there. It had a keister in it. We were having quite a bit of trouble with it and we didn't realize how much time had gone by. Both of us were working on it because there was no place for a point man.

We knew that the janitor got there about four o'clock in the morning. On this occasion he came down a little early and he had another guy with him. We heard the front door close and we heard him coming up the stairs. I told Bad-Eye that we would just have to hold them up before they got to the light switch. Well, I don't carry a pistol. But I had a short bar that was sawed off on one end. I put it under my arm so that just the end of it stuck out. When this janitor and his partner showed up I just stepped out and told them to stick them up. They put their hands up and turned their backs. We then tied them up. I often wonder if they knew that I didn't have a pistol.

It usually takes a three-man crew to work, although a two-man crew can work. There are these friends of mine that just came into town and that's a two-man crew. That's just a point man there, because both of them are very capable. One time one of them will open the box and the next time the other will open it.

You become tired of openin' after a while; it ceases to be a novelty, I guess, whatever; it's just the case of openin' the box and gettin' the money. You have the utmost trust in your partner so you never worry about whether you're gonna get first count of the money or if he's gonna fill his pockets before he brings it out. If you haven't got that confidence in him, then you don't work with him. But a three-man crew is more common because quite often you have to move the box out from the wall in order to get to it if it's a round-door. There's only one practical means of entry to it and in order to drill it you have to move it out from the wall. If it's a large round-door, which most of the supermarkets have, they weigh a ton, and you have to have someone to help you work in there and you can't use your point man. So that's why it's more practical to have a three-man crew. That way you can get all boxes, you have no problems and you're working enough so it will support a three-man crew if you're a good box man.

I got $19,000 one time in San Francisco and afterwards we went to a nightclub and closed up the bar and in a few days I didn't have anything. I never left the bar. We just closed the front door and I just told them to shut up the doors and blow this and I just kept throwing money on the bar and everybody who was in there stayed right there. We stayed there twenty-four hours a day. With that kind of money the owner would chance staying closed twenty-four hours a day. He just locked the door and everybody just stayed right there. We just sent out for food, I guess. That was about the most foolish thing I ever did. But a box man almost always is foolish with money. It all depends on the guy. Just like anybody else, one guy might save some of it, the other guy blows it as fast as he makes it. I could have saved quite a bit of mine so I wouldn't have to work too often. But I hit a town and I know the town was gonna catch on fire in a little bit so I'll really burn her up. I'd help set her on fire and I'd root like mad for a little bit and back off. I'm shakin' the dice all the time that this ain't my night to sneeze so we keep on rootin'.

The average box man doesn't save any money. I had a partner that anytime that we'd make a score, he'd fly to Reno and three days later he's broke. We're all suckers for somethin', I guess. The average box man can work, oh, every three months and do all right and live very good, too. I know some box men that have to work every couple of weeks. Because they blow it in bars and stuff like that. Chicks. After making a score I may have planned a trip back East maybe, and these friends of mine who are back there now in Montana, they just came out of North Dakota. Well they just leisurely cruise across the country, you know, and if they find a score on the way over that's dandy. If they don't, why they go to where they're going to root because they've got a score back in Montana and they are on their way back now.

But they just monkey around comin' back a little bit and they call me two, three times and want to know if there's any heat on around here and I check for them and find out if there is or isn't. Maybe they desire to go to the Mardi Gras or something. You see when they leave here they don't know where they're goin'. I mean, they live out of a suitcase. They have no home, really. And both these guys keep an apartment here all the time year in and year out—they pay a year's rent on a lease, each one of them; they live in different areas of the town—harder to check on that way. The average guy just says, "Man I'm getting tired of here, the heat's on here, let's go." So you go.

Maybe you want to go to Canada or something and you go up there. I always had trouble trading the money in so I don't like Canada. You have to give an awful big discount on the money.

We had a poison joint that we could not find the box in, so after looking it over several times I decided to take it but I took no safe tools as I was sure there was no safe—imagine my surprise after getting in to find a box over in the corner behind a big old wood burning stove and me with no tools. There was a double bitted axe in the wood box so I decided to try and open it with the axe. And I did, even to my surprise. I entered into the toilet room and while stepping down from the water closet to the seat my foot slipped and I spent the evening working with one wet foot.

I never got along very well in Seattle 'cause we used to run into Seattle and root, and run back out again, and the bulls knew it but they couldn't do nothing about it. We'd be long gone; we'd be back in Portland by the time they found out their box had been beaten.

But sometimes it's rather hard. A town can get real hot.

I specialized in supermarkets 'cause outside of a bank that was the only place where they had large amounts of money. We couldn't get to and from the caper very easily, so we'd look around for somebody that could get us there. Cab drivers, they got a bad reputation; they tell everything they know. Once we used a policeman, a prowl car. It worked pretty good. He'd take us out there and then he listens on his radio and he goes down by a pay phone. He stays near this pay phone and he dials the number of this supermarket right up to the last digit, and that will hold the line open. All he has to do is to jump in there and flip that last number and that will start ringing the phone in there. Well, at two or three o'clock in the morning, I don't think there is any woman calling up wanting to know if her kid's in the store or something. It's got to be that policeman, that's all there is to it. So when we hear that phone we go. And you tear out of there and you've got a predetermined place where you'll meet him. You have two or three of by where you are going to get picked up. He comes along and picks you up, and we drive right by the bulls that are surrounding the store and go on about our business.

Ninety percent of the police department isn't crooked. I don't say that by any means. But I would venture to say that there's a few thieves everywhere. That's the same with the police department. You can't put a group of people together without somebody's going to be crooked.

I pulled in this small town and looked around for a mark. Only thing that looked good was the local poolroom but the box sat right in the front window. While walking down the street I saw a wrecker and I went in the poolroom and put a chain around the box and my partner backed the wrecker up to the window and I hooked the chain onto the cable of the wrecker. It was a nice score, too.

While working on a supermarket one night we noticed a large number of prowl cars running around. They did not disturb us; we completed our work and went home and the next morning we read where a safe man had been working down a block from us and got a rank, which put all the heat in the neighborhood as the guy had gotten away.

I was in this place working once when I saw the cop looking in the door. He unlocked the door and came in with his pistol in hand and in his stance and walk I knew he would pump six shots into anything that moved. I could feel and smell death that night. But he went out without seeing me.

One time we had just made an entry into this department store and laid our tools out to go to work and the point man was getting ready to get on the point when we heard someone come in the front door. The box was on the balcony and we laid on the floor and watched the town-clown [local policeman] go all over the first floor but he never came near the box. Just before he left he went over and picked up three or four articles and stuck them in his pocket and went out—we continued with our work. We would have left if he had just gone out but we knew when he clouted this stuff that we had no rank.

I got a rank from the town-clown in a small town. He just up and shot at me and hit me in the belly. I got away and made it to my car. I drove all the way to Portland and got hold of a croaker [doctor] I knew who checked me in the hospital. The three slugs had not hurt any-thing—maybe I had no guts to hurt. They dug the slugs out and that's all there was to it. I went home in a couple of days, as soon as they give me back the amount of blood I had lost.

We heard that a real estate office had taken in a large sum of money so we went to get it. I stood point and my partner loaded the box with grease—when it was all clear he let her go and he had over-loaded—the whole door blew off and come sailing out through the plate glass window. It had turned so it was flat and revolving slowly as it came out the window. I was so surprised I just stood there and looked at it drop to the middle of the street with a loud clang. Lights came on all over the neighborhood and my partner came flying out—but he had stayed long enough to get the loot.

One of the cutest scores was when we cut up through the floor of this place and while my partner was picking up the tools I went over and looked at the box. I saw that the crack around the door was extra wide. I stuck my screwdriver in and pried. The door came open. I took out the money sacks and turned to my partner who was still gathering tools. I asked him if he was going to stay all night. To this day he thinks I am the greatest and fastest box man there is.

One night we had to kidnap a box—we had to steal the whole safe. It was sittin' in front of a window so we couldn't open it; it was just a small box. There was a guy named Dick Shopus; he's dead; he was a chief of dicks [Chief of Police Detectives] in Portland and he was a dirty rotten bugger; boy he was really rotten. He takes money from guys and then, you know, double-crosses them. It only took us a few minutes to open the box after we got it out. We had it in the back of the car and we was goin' down to dump it in the river. We got lost by accident in this Dick Shopus's neighborhood and I asked this kid that was with me, "Say don't Dick live around here?" and he says, "Yeah," and I says, "Let's go by his house." So we go by his house and he had just seeded his front lawn. So we took the safe out and dumped it on his front lawn. Then we called the *Oregonian* and told them if they wanted to get a good picture for the morning edition to go out to Dick Shopus's house, and they did. The next morning the picture was on the front page. And incidentally, every safe-man left town the next day. But I had a perverted sense of humor so I enjoyed seeing the headlines with a picture of the safe in his front yard.

You have quite a sense of accomplishment, you know, in beating the police. They set up all these traps to get you and it's quite an accomplishment, just like any job. It's exciting, and I really believe that it's the excitement that makes it appealing. I think, watching these kids the excitement that makes it appealing. I think, watching these kids today, some of them I've worked with, that it's just the excitement that they see, the thrill of it. But after a while you settle down. You need the money, that's all.

One time I ran into a little trouble with the bulls up and down the coast and so we went and bought a truck and trailer, the other guy and I. I almost had to kill him to get him to go into it and I wasn't sure enough about it to confide him my plans, so I was thinking up some crazy thing so he went along with me anyhow. We bought this truck and trailer and started riding up and down the coast here. We'd contract to haul stuff so it looked like we was honest. But we started looking for marks. And we'd pull up—truck and trailer would cover up a half of a block—and I'd park the truck in front of the joint and go and knock off a joint and bulls can't see in it, you know. Come out and get in the truck and drive off. We fooled them for quite a while there. But the fact that you go on 99, Seattle to Los Angeles, you know, there's some smart cop who finally begins to say, "Well, it's funny all these are happening on 99 and, you know, from Seattle to Los Angeles." And somebody says, "Well, that sounds like a truck." So we watched them. We see them begin to check the trucks out and then we got rid of ours. We'd played it out. But you have to think of things like that. You have to think of things like that or else you don't succeed.

If I was rootin', you know, and the bulls in Portland were giving me a bad time, why, I'd come up to Seattle and live. And go down to Portland and knock off the boxes and then laugh at 'em. I'd get a lot of enjoyment out of it. I'd have a bull here telling me what's going on, how they're burning up that teletype and everything; then I'd just be giving the Bronx cheer all the time. We'd enjoy that you know.

There was one score that the bulls never forgave me for. In fact they sent me to prison because of it though it had to be for a different caper 'cause they couldn't ever prove I did it. We went down and kidnapped a fork-lift and a truck. The box was sitting right in the front window of this great big store. And there were five different police agencies within a block—the state police, two different county sheriffs' departments, the city police and the door-shakers were all within a block of this store. This place was right at the county line where all these bulls just sit around and talk. We took the truck down and lifted the safe right out of the window just quick, quick, quick. It went perfect just like I said it would. I mean, we felt pretty proud of that, you know.

The kid who worked the caper with me asked me if he could drive out there the next morning and watch the action. I said, "Sure, go ahead." You know, I didn't dare go 'cause they would have thrown me in jail—they would have been so mad they would have thrown me in on general principles and sent me to the joint for it. But he went out there and wandered around because they didn't know that he was a box man.

I always used to teach my partners to tell the bulls that they were a milk bottle—doormat-thief. Don't let them know you're a box man because that's the most feared criminal there is to the police department. 'Cause they never see them. They haven't anything to go on. No witnesses or anything. And that makes it awful hard to catch them. And that kid—till the day we got pinched—they never did know he was a box man and they were dumbfounded. When the kid came back he told me they was going crazy. They took fingerprints off of anything but the milk bottles in the ash box that morning—to get a lead. And the door-shaker had a big special police dog and when he'd arrive at one of his locations that he was protecting, he'd let the dog out of the car and the dog would run around the building and smell for fresh scent. And we had the dog beat 'cause we went way down, way down here on the roof. It was in a center—one of these centers—we went way down here where he didn't shake the door. Went on the roof down there so the dog wouldn't pay no attention to us. We went along the roof all the way down to the store we wanted to go in. We never told him how we got on the roof, and he figured that the dog was no good so he sold him.

There were lots of things like that that were interesting, you know, to accomplish. The same as anyone else, you want to become the best in your field. Not necessarily the best, but you want to be good. So I studied it hard. Worked hard at it. I worked real hard at it. And I was one of the best in the country, I guess, on the West Coast, but it's like one time we wanted to burn a box down here, I kept thinking, man, there's been a lot of guys that got a beef from buying something locally, you know. So I got a friend of mine who was going to Texas and I told him exactly what to buy and what I wanted and he got my torches down there.

One night here in Seattle I got a drugstore that surprised me. I did something that I disliked doing very much. I opened the safe up, got the money out, and here was about a dozen watches in there. I just put them in with the money. I got over to the motel and I looked at these watches. They were real old antiques. We handled them and opened them up. I was very afraid that I couldn't erase all the finger prints so we didn't dare put them in anything and send them back to the guy. I tried to think of some way of getting them back to him because I felt bad about taking them. So we had to end up throwing them in the lake. It has always bothered me that I had to destroy something like that which was an antique.

Bad-Eye and I took a trip into California one time with another guy that had the nickname of Budweiser. Budweiser was an old-time box man. We missed this caper down there. We had spent quite a bit of effort on it too. It was in the department store and something went wrong. We came back and the next day Budweiser went up to Bad-Eye's apartment and gave him a bad time. That afternoon I had an appointment with Bad-Eye and he didn't show up for the appointment. I went up to his apartment and talked with his wife. She told me that she hadn't seen him since that morning. She was his common-law wife; she was a prostitute. On a hunch I called Jim and asked him to check. The story came out that Bad-Eye had gotten pretty unhappy with the way Bud had acted that morning. So he went up to the hotel that afternoon before he had this meeting with me to cool off this Budweiser. Bad-Eye knocked on the door and Bud answered. Bad-Eye asked if he could come in. Budweiser said no. He started calling Bad-Eye a bunch of names. All of a sudden he pulled this butcher knife out from behind him and took a swing at Bad-Eye. Bad-Eye caught it on his hand. He was mad then. I was surprised to hear this because he was a very mild guy normally. He got this knife away from Budweiser and he stabbed him and killed him. There wouldn't have been anything to it if Bad-Eye had stayed still. But he didn't; he ran. We had a hell of a time locating him. By that time they had brought a manslaughter charge against him. There was so much publicity involved in it that he had to go to the joint and do five years on it.

Bad-Eye wasn't a hype but he played around with a lot of stuff. He and I had a lot of fun together rooting. Both of us had no worries. We would go crack some poison joints and he would get enough stuff [drugs] to last him two or three months. Then we would go out and root for money. He was pretty smart but he had a perverted sense of humor. One time we needed some grease, nitroglycerin, to use on a caper. I said that I hadn't any because I hadn't used any for a long while. He said that he had some. We went down to a little town one night that was outside of Portland. We went out in this high school yard. I asked him where he had this grease planted. He said that he would show me. We had taken a shovel with us. We went over to the goal post of the football field and dug around there and dug up the grease. Remember that this is where the kids play football all the time and that's where he had the stuff planted. I tried to explain to him that I thought this was outrageous. Kids could get blown up because the grease was very touchy. Any sharp blow would set it off. He just laughed and thought nothing of it.

We went on a trip one time with grease and you have to keep it warm all the time. If you let it get too cold it gets touchy, and the older it gets the more touchy it gets. Usually we keep it in our pants right inside of our belt against our bodies to let the body temperature take care of it. That was sufficient to keep it from going off. We went down to this department store which was in the northern part of California. In the back of the store was an alley. There was a sloping shed roof that we could climb up on and jimmy the window to get into the building. Bad-Eye went up first while I stood point for him out in the alley. Remember that I have the grease stuck in my pants. Bad-Eye's got what we call the bonnets, the caps that are used to set the grease off. After he has this window opened, I reached up to grab a hold of the gutter on the edge of this roof in order to pull myself up. When I did this I sucked my gut in. When I sucked my gut in, it released this bottle of grease, which slid down my pants leg. You can believe that I was paralyzed. It just slid down my pants leg and hit me in the instep and then it slid on the ground. If it had hit the pavement it would have gone off. But hitting my instep kept it from having a sharp blow. I think I was as scared then as I ever was in my life.

One night with Bad-Eye we went to beat a poison joint. At that time I was working on a salary for Jim and rooting for narcotics for him. I told Bad-Eye that I first had to make a score for narcotics before we did anything further. He said that he would help me. He was very congenial along those lines. Of course he got half interest on the money that was in there. So we went down to this poison joint and we had never cased it. But we locked it up that night. That means that we stayed there and watched the guy lock up and go home. Now this guy had been beat before so he was pretty smart. He locked up the front door, went home, had dinner, came back to the store, went in the back door and slept in the store. We were watching the front of the store. We saw him leave and we tailed him home. We saw him go into his house and that's what we call putting them to bed. So we knew that it was perfectly safe. We went back there and laid on it in case he came back. But he never came in the front door; he came in by the back door. We went in through the skylight, dropped down by a rope into the building; but something seemed wrong to me. Of course we don't talk when we are working. We are extremely quiet. We never dreamed that there was anybody in the place. This was about two in the morning. I motioned to Bad-Eye to be quiet, that I sensed that there was something wrong. I crawled around on my hands and knees and I could hear breathing. I located where the breathing was coming from and I opened the door up and looked in there. My eyes were used to the dark by that time and the street lights threw enough light for me to see this guy in bed there. Right beside the bed is a chair and leaning against the chair is a shotgun, a double-barrel one. We knew that the guy was old and that he was harmless if he didn't have his shotgun. So we removed the shotgun and took the shells out of it and set the gun back in there. We robbed the place of the narcotics and as we left out the back door we slammed the door real hard. We waited up the alley about four hundred feet and sure enough the old guy comes running out the back door with his shotgun. We let him see us. He was in his nightshirt by the way. He put the shotgun up to his shoulder and shouted to us to stop. He pulled both triggers, which would have blasted us down if there had been any shots in there. I bet he felt silly when nothing happened. I always wanted to go back and ask him what he thought when the gun didn't go off.

At that time I was living with an ex-prostitute. She quit being a prostitute when she moved in with me because I made enough money so that she didn't have to work. And I didn't want her to work. Right down the street from where we lived there was a store; it had three check stands, owned by an old German. My old lady kept telling me that I should see all the money in the square box. This box was situated in such a manner that it was flush with the wall, facing the store. The safe was in the warehouse part. She kept picking away at me. I never told her that I was a box man, but she knew I was. Sometimes I would be gone on trips and wouldn't get back for a week or so. I would leave in the evening and wouldn't get back until the next morning and I would have a lot of money and would be tired and dirty. She would have to be stupid if she didn't know these things were going on.

She kept picking away at me about this box so I said the hell with it and decided to go get it. I went down and went into the warehouse. I was by myself. It was what we called a cold caper. There were no windows in the warehouse. I decided to open the safe from the back. In order to open it from the back you had to take the whole sheet of iron off and then dig out the concrete. Then the safe is lined with wood. You have to dig all this wood out. Consequently all the shelves come out and drawers and everything else. When you get through the safe is in shambles. Well I had to tear all of this out in order to get to the money. I cleaned the safe out completely. I went home and told her that here was money for her to buy a fur coat or something. She thought that over and guessed that I had probably gotten the money from the store. The next morning she gets up bright and early and heads down to the store. Sure enough, while she's in the store the owner goes and opens up the safe. She tells me about it when she gets home and she's all excited. He opens up the safe and he looks in and he's looking into the warehouse. There is nothing in the safe. She said that he crawled clear in that safe. She demonstrated all of this to me. We both just about died laughing. But I never admitted that I got it. I never did admit those things to anybody.

The only time thieves discuss capers is with another thief that they have worked with for a long time. But you couldn't trust these women with things like that. They are likely to get mad at you and tell somebody else about something and two minutes later they are sorry they did it. But the trouble has already started. It's too late then to bring it back. So you just don't tell them anything.

Bad-Eye and I did a lot of exploration work, I guess that is what you would call it. We would find places like an insurance company one time. It was quite a large insurance company and we couldn't find out from any of the other box men if insurance companies had money in them or not. We thought the most simple thing to do would be to break into one and find out. We broke into this one that had a vault in it. In knocking the combination off we bent the spindle. The spindle is the shaft that is attached to the combination. It was an old Pacific coast vault, what is called a punch box. You could punch them out with a punch. You didn't have to peel or burn them. When we knocked them off we bent the spindle a little bit. I bet we spent four hours trying to punch that box when it normally would have been three minutes. I told Bad-Eye fifty times that it wasn't worth it. But he insisted; he wanted to get in that vault. We got in it; there was a nominal amount of money, I don't recall how much was in it. We got it and went home.

One thing that you must understand is that professional criminals trust one another, to the extent that Bad-Eye and I used to argue about who was going to take the money home. Each one of us was insistent that the other guy take it home. That meant that the guy that took it home had to roll the coins up and take them down to the bank, changing them for paper. We would always argue about who would take the money home. We trusted one another completely for an honest split, which we got from one another. I never gave it a thought to beat Bad-Eye and I'm sure he never thought to beat me anytime.

One night Bad-Eye and I went down to get a country store, groceries, meat, hardware and everything. They were rather lucrative stores. They all had what we called a square box in them. We went down to beat it and it was pouring down rain. We went around to our means of entry and lo and behold the glass was gone out of the door. I stood there and thought it over; Bad-Eye was still in the car. It just didn't make sense to me. There wasn't even a door-shaker in this town. They had a town-clown who went home about midnight. I thought it over and over and finally I took a chance and I turned my flashlight inside the store. There were wet footprints in there. I went back to Bad-Eye and asked him if we should run the bastards off or just forget about it. We decided to forget about it because neither one of us were carrying guns. I thought that was a terrific coincidence that two different sets of thieves would decide to rob a place on the same night. It was the only time in my life that a situation like that came up.

I worked with a young kid once. His name was Leonard. I worked with him for quite awhile. I didn't like it because he had to be told everything. You had to take him by the hand; he had no imagination. I always felt that he had a certain amount of fear in him. You just can't have any fear, that plugs up your mind. Your mind has to be open all the time. You have to be like an animal and be on your toes all the time prepared for danger that might arise. If you have a fear in you when you start, it plugs up a part of your mind. It's not good. Like you cannot have any animosity toward the police department because you are likely to be laying on a joint and a patrol car will go by. That animosity will subconsciously come up and it plugs up your mind. Your mind should be calm all the time and thinking about how those bulls are thinking and if they are alerted to anything. I could never teach Leonard not to have any animosity. Bad-Eye had no animosity; he was smart enough for that. Denver Dick had no animosity.

We didn't like the policemen. We despised them, but we never let it plug up our mind at any time where it became harmful. Now Leonard would do that. He would often become frightened. Like an animal, he was likely to run in any direction once he was frightened. In my case, I would know exactly in what direction I was going to run all the time. All I did was to watch the police car very closely to see what their reaction was.

I didn't stay with Leonard for too long. Then I was with a guy named Buster. He was a full-fledged hype. Buster would do most anything as long as in the end he could see narcotics. It didn't matter whether you were stealing the narcotics or whether you stole the money to obtain the narcotics. One night there was a clinic that had several doctors' offices in it. We decided to get it. We went out there and I put him in the reception room, which had a big bay-window right out into the street. I went in and went to work on the safe. According to my figures, there should have been a fair amount of narcotics in there and a good sum of money. I'm working on this box and I smell something burning. I'm not burning with a torch that night; I'm peeling the box. I knew it wasn't a cigarette because I don't smoke while I work because I perspire so much. I kept smelling this. I quit work and tried to trail down where this smoke was coming from. I walked into the reception room and here is Buster. He has got canvas gloves on and he is leaning up against the side of the window. He is supposed to be on the point. He is holding a cigarette in his hand. He is so knocked down on narcotics that this cigarette is igniting his glove, which was smoldering. He doesn't have the faintest idea that his glove is on fire. That terminated my business with Buster.

I joined a kid named Danny who had a lot of guts. He used to be a fighter. I liked Danny real well. He was a pimp, which all of them guys were. He knew nothing about safes and I taught him. We got along fine. I had to do all the work, get the tools and everything. He had no ambition; all he wanted to do was to knock the joint off. He soon grew out of hand and began thinking that he was capable of casing these joints. Casing the joint is an enormous job. You have to have considerable experience to be able to decide whether there is any money involved in the place, whether they keep it there all night or whether they take it with them, and things like that. Well Danny decided that he was very capable. He picked out two or three scores. I would go look at this score and could see that it was a bum one. But I would go along with him and go and open it. There would be a couple hundred dollars in there and that's all. It didn't seem to bother him. He still thought he was capable of picking these scores out.

One of the good things about working with Danny was that he was honest with me. He always saw to it that we had an equal division of the money, and he was always willing to work. The only thing he lacked was the experience. He had no previous experience until I took him under my wing and taught him. In fact he and I went to Salem together on a caper. It was Danny who messed up a real good caper.

I had looked at this place and it had a round door safe in it. I designed a dolly and had it built with four wheels on it and a frame. This supermarket was one of a chain. They had their own trucks. We went down to the warehouse and stole one of the company trucks. We had a detective harnessed up, fixed, and he was our point man.

We got in and got the safe tipped over on the dolly—it was all concrete enclosed. We moved it out to the back door and I sent Danny over to get the truck, which was parked a few blocks away. It was in the winter time and the motor was cold. He was banging this motor around and the truck was backfiring. The he woke somebody up across the street from the parking lot. They called the police. Just as he backed up the truck to the platform the telephone started ringing. I said, come on, I think we have time to shove it on there. I hadn't noticed that he hadn't completely backed the truck up to the platform; there was a gap of about six inches. The wheels on the dolly wouldn't jump this six inches. The safe hit this crack and went down between the truck and the platform and we had to run away and leave it.

We heard about this guy who had bought a large amount of diamonds that were unset from back East and was going to sell them legitimately in Portland. We decided to beat him. One of the guys had seen the diamonds. We broke into the place by cutting a hole through the roof. I wa waiting for it to get almost daylight before I started to work. The paper boy came along, lifted up the mail slot, shoved the paper in. Danny runs in and says we have a rank and so we take off from the joint and leave. We had cut a hole through the roof so that ruined that mark. After we got home I asked Danny where the rank came from. I was in the back end of this warehouse so I didn't see or hear what had happened. After he had told me what had happened, that the boy had come up and shook the door, I got in my car and drove down there. Here in the front door was the newspaper. I pushed the mail slot and it made a noise. I knew that was what ruined the caper.

In the old days we had what we called the Australian slang. It is used in the joint. If it is talked real fast, you can't understand it. We used to stand right in front of guards and talk it. They would get very unhappy and tell us to cut it out. The only phrase that I can remember is "Piper hizek, the bottles and stoppers walking down the fields of wheat on the right chalk." When you say that fast it is hard to interpret it. What it means is: Piper hizek—look; bottles and stoppers— which is copper instead of bulls (cops); walking down the fields of wheat—the street; on the right chalk—which is the sidewalk. Things like lump of lead is head, north and south is mouth. A true professional criminal very seldom uses a slang outside of a terminology that is used in his particular livelihood such as safecracking. They never call it a safe but a pete or a box. They have names like spindle and gutbox. Outside of an institution they don't talk Australian slang because they never talk in front of anybody. They just talk between the two of them.

One of the reasons why I think I have such little respect for society is that the majority of things like jewelry and furs that we had an occasion to steal from rich people we always sold to legitimate dealers. People say fences are underworld characters. Well that is not altogether true. I have dealt with underworld characters but in the majority of cases the people were legitimate. Well up in society and in the town. They couldn't resist making that extra dollar from us guys.

One night I went out with this partner. This joint was bugged up; it was a poison joint, a drugstore. I figured out how to cut through the roof and into the ceiling and beat the bug. I cut the hole in the roof with an expansion bit and a keyhole saw. We took an umbrella with us when we went out on this type of caper. We cut a small hole, just big enough for the umbrella to slip through. Then we reached down in there and opened up the umbrella. The we knocked all the plaster loose and the hole was then big enough for our bodies to go through. The plaster falls into the umbrella. Otherwise all that dust would hang in the air. In a quiet store like that there is no draft to carry it away. If the door-shaker goes by and happens to turn the spotlight in there they can see that dust and they know that something is wrong. I told my partner that I would put the rope down and that he was to slip down the rope. I dropped the rope down in there. On the floor was what you would call islands, round counters. It was a long store and it had an island down the center. He got about halfway down the rope and then he fell on one of the islands and knocked it over. He was laying on the floor moaning. Then I dropped down there with the tools. Instead of going to him and seeing what was wrong with him, I went over and started sweeping all these toothbrushes that flew out in the aisle and that could be seen from the door. I went and opened up the box and got all the money and narcotics out of it. All my partner moaned about for the next week was that I was more interested in sweeping the toothbrushes out of the aisle than I was in his health. He thought he had a broken leg, but he didn't.

4

The Rackets

*"The Rackets is run just like legitimate
business . . .
there's a lot of conniving . . .
they get the fix in and they get double-
crossed . . .
but they take care of it before its over
with. . . ."*

The worst thing that you can do is open up a town to gambling, prostitution and things like that. I shouldn't say this because there's a lot
of legitimate people make their living at it. But everyone hollers,
"Open the town up." And I look at these square-johns and think "You
damn fool." Now is this sensible? The minute you open that town up
the thieves come in, see, so they're going to move into the town and
these fools are talking about how closing the town throws card-deal-
ers out of work, and stuff like that. The minute you open up the town
and let a thing like that in, bang, the thieves are going to move in. Because they all belong to the same association, you know. Larceny is
coming out of them. And if you're going to shut it down, shut it down
tight, no worries, no nothing.

I don't know the answer to it. Because you've got to have prostitution, I guess, because they've had it since the beginning of time. But
how they're going to answer it without getting thieves in town, I don't
know. A lot of towns have it—they'll give a pimp a year everytime
they catch him on the street for no reason, and they'll run them all out
of town. It only takes a week for them to all find that out. The word
goes out, "Don't go to Seattle man—you'll get a year." Well, that
keeps them out. In fact, I can run all the thieves out of this town. Any
police force can. All they have to do is anytime they catch a thief on
the street lock him up. I don't care if he's in his home or what; you can

believe that that thief is going to go someplace else and steal, you know. But the police don't run them out of town, why, I don't know. They just let them stay.

I worked in the rackets [prostitution, gambling, drug peddling] in Portland some years back. I worked for a guy named Jim who took over the town.

I was a bag-man one time in Portland. A guy named Jack and I managed all the slot machines in the nightclubs. Jack and I would start out at 11:00 at night and we would make all the clubs, slot machines, lottery joints. We would then count up the cash. We would check the slot machines out and all the whiskey in the clubs, the gambling games in the clubs. All our clubs were in the downtown area. Jim let other operators run clubs in the outskirts of town and they paid off so much a month. The same with the whorehouses. We didn't run any of the whorehouses personally; we leased them out to landladies or, rather, we furnished protection to these landladies, and then they would pay off. Jack's and my job was to collect from all the clubs every night and then the first of the month we would go out and collect from all the whorehouses and the outlying clubs.

We had the only slot machines that were allowed to run in town. So any of these clubs that had slots in them—whorehouses, bookies, lottery joints—would have to use our slot machines, which we checked every night. This was because guys were continuously raiding us and breaking the machines or taking them out of the town and selling them. We bought truck loads of machines from as far away as Montana. Guys would hijack them over there and when they got a truck load of them they would sell them to us.

When I first went to work for Jim in Portland a guy named Emlou owned the slot machines at that time. He was quite a high roller. He would go out and get drunk and light his cigar with hundred dollar bills. He was actually just a local country boy who fell heir to this empire. So Jim's brother Fred went to work for Emlou. I don't remember what his capacity was. Fred was a pimp too. Fred and Jim discussed taking the town away from Emlou. I was there in the slot machine warehouse the day they came down and took over. I knew something was cooking for some time but I didn't know exactly what it was. They never did discuss it with me.

Jim walked in with a double-barrel sawed off shotgun and I'll never forget it. Fred went in the office and told Emlou that they were taking over. One of the slot machine mechanics got scared and started to leave. Jim took the shotgun, reached out with it stuck it between his legs and tripped him. He was very calm and collected with no excitement or nothing. He just told the guys that from then on they were working for him. That's the way it was. Emlou was out. No money changed hands or anything.

That was in the days of lottery joints, nightclubs: there were a lot of slot machines in operation. Everybody had them operating. Stores, lottery joints, gambling joints, bootleg joints—almost any place you could think of. American Legion, Elks, Veterans Club, all of them had machines. They were all operated by Jim.

I went to work for Jim and Fred. I didn't care too much for Fred. But Jim was a likable guy. He and I did a lot of stealing together. We were hungry a few times when they shut the town down on him before he got complete control of it. So there were both good and bad times.

We used to go out and steal and keep our tools in the warehouse, which was all agreeable with Jim. Sometimes we would give him some money and sometimes we wouldn't. But he was making so much money then that he didn't mind and he liked me.

With his connections in the police department, which he inherited from Emlou, he gradually built it up until he had full control of the department. He got a chief appointed. He was a figurehead if there ever was one. He didn't know nothing about police work but Jim got him appointed chief. Nobody got a promotion around there without Jim's OK first. We paid terrific sums to the police and judges. I know we had an awful payoff to make every month. Exactly how much was actually paid off, I don't know. I know that everybody seemed to get a piece of it. We were paying off every beat bull up to the chief of police.

Then Jim went into city council. He got a couple of the city councilmen elected, which made him strong with the city council. By that time he was the boss. We had all the gambling joints, all the bootleg joints in the downtown area, and nobody could open up any place without an OK from Jim. He could square almost any beef except a murder beef, which none of us were involved with. We operated openly; nothing was hidden at all. We carried our tools around in the open because we worked for Jim. We could double park our car out in the middle of the street and let it sit there. The cops wouldn't dare touch it because we worked for Jim.

One time I went to Salem with Jim while he went in and visited the supreme court judges there. He told them how to make a decision in such and such a case.

We had four or five guys who were all goons that we kept in the office all the time. Whenever there was any trouble in one of the lottery joints or clubs we would get this gang and go down there and cool them off. Quite often we would have to give a dumping [a beating] to whoever was causing the trouble. In the lottery joints it was the longshoremen who caused all the trouble. These longshoremen would carry these hooks that they used in handling cargo. They would get mad at the machine and sink the hook into the front of the machine and tear the whole front out of it. That way they would get the jackpot. Usually, it was because they were drunk or because they were angry for not winning. We had the machines tightened up so that they would pay off loosely or tightly, either one. In fact, you can fix them so that they never pay off a jackpot. The customer can't tell the difference; it doesn't show.

We had about ten bootleg nightclubs running at that time. Part of my duties were to ride around with a guy named Jack, who we called Pencil. He was very sharp; he could figure percentages real good. Every night we made the collections from all these clubs. He would figure up the percentages of the whiskey used and collect from the club manager who was always some kind of a thief who would try to beat him if he could. But Jack was a pretty smart kid. My job was to ride with Jack the Pencil and protect him. By the time we got through we would have quite a large amount of money to take back to the office.

It was during the time that we had this office and warehouse that I wanted to become acquainted with the burglary alarms. So I talked to Jim about it and we had one of them put in. So we had an ADT system, which was considered the best at that time, installed in the warehouse. When they got through putting it in I had already figured out how to beat it. I often used this knowledge later. Jim was considered legitimate so ADT never thought anything about installing this system there.

It was during payday that several different guys came to Jim and wanted to buy in with him. So he would always sell the business to them. They would give him cash for it. He would sell them the business and say he would fix it with the police so they could operate. They would pay him for the joint and us guys would know what the score was. Jim would sell this slot machine operation to some clown. The guy would run it for a couple of weeks and then the bulls would come and tell them that the town was too hot: such and such a church is screaming so you will have to shut down. So they would shut him down. Then the first of the month would come and the bulls would come around and tell him to open up. He would make the payoff first and then he would go ahead and open up. He would operate for three days and then they would tell him that he would have to shut down. This went on for two or three payoff periods and then the guy would get smart to the fact that he was being had. He would go to Jim and tell him that he wanted his money back and that he didn't want to continue with it. Jim would tell him that he had spent the money and couldn't give it back to him and that he didn't want the machines. The guy would go around and try to sell it to someone else. But everyone was too smart to buy it because they knew what the score was. So nobody would buy it. So there the guy is with a warehouse full of machines; he has the upkeep and the mechanics, paying off the bulls and everything. He finally would just give up. In the contract that Jim had made him sign, if he didn't do this or that, then Jim got the outfit back. Jim did this five or six times that I know of. These guys were considered pretty smart people in their own operation. But as soon as they tangled with Jim he would make a fool of them.

We had to watch the mechanics in the slots very closely and the dealers in the gambling joints, the bartenders in the clubs. All of them were thieves in one form or another. Jim had to keep on his toes at all times to keep up with them. They would try to steal him blind. Sometimes we solved it by just talking to them and sometimes they had the fear in them beforehand and they didn't attempt to do anything. Sometimes we had to give them a dumping.

That's where the goons come in. Some night when these guys went home, the goon would be parked in front of their house. He would get a royal dumping. Ten to one he wouldn't even know who gave it to him. If he would get smart Jim would tell him that maybe he had it coming to him. The guy would wake up to the fact that it was part of the deal that we sent the guy out. But he could never prove it. Usually, the guy would go back to work and keep his nose clean. Some of them didn't and they would get two or three dumpings before they finally woke up.

Fred, Jim's brother, had all the whorehouses in Portland. He controlled them all. He didn't have the landladies, he just controlled the whorehouses. Instead of them paying off the police department directly, they just paid Fred off. Then Fred paid the police department through Jim. The landladies gave up a certain percentage of their earnings. If it looked like they dropped down he would just tell the bulls to shut them down. The bulls would have a raid and pinch the girls. The landlady would have to bail the girls out and go to court. If she didn't get in line and become honest about her payoff then this would happen quite regularly.

I never had anything to do with the whorehouses. I was known to all the landladies, that I was close to Jim and that I could have anything that I wanted out of them. But I had no interest or desire to hang around them. Not being a pimp, there was no reason for me to hang around them. Fred controlled that exclusively, except when we had to call the goon out and then that went through Jim's end of it.

One time a mob from Minneapolis decided to move into Portland. At that time we had closed down all the clubs except one. I don't recall why we closed them down. We had this one enormous club that was very profitable. The Eastern syndicate from Minneapolis sent a guy out and he just declared himself in. Like I said, Jim was a very smart person. He said, alright you are in. That's all there is to it. I'm not going to fight you. So he went down to the police department and told them that this guy was in town and that he represented this Eastern mob and did they want this mob in there. They said no, that they were very happy with the situation the way it was. This guy used to sit in the club all day and part of the night. He would check the books and everything to make sure they got their end of it. Jim tried every way in the world to get rid of him. He had the town shut down completely. This guy waited it out. He had nothing to loose. He was living off the earnings that he got out of the club. He figured that he would just sit there and wait. He was reporting by phone all the time to his bosses back East.

The cops tried shutting down the clubs and opening them up again. Jim grew tried of that. We went down and burnt the club down one night, which actually was a very small loss to us. The building was insured and everything. Jim profited from that. He didn't mind because he got rid of the guy. This guy called up his bosses right in front of Jim. He told them that they didn't have a chance, that it was snowballing there. The guy from Minneapolis was pretty smart. He knew that we had burnt it down. He knew he wasn't going to win any more arguments. He hadn't declared in with the police department, they weren't accepting him. So he left and went back East. To my knowledge, that's the only time that we had an outside syndicate try to move in until the Teamsters tried to take over.

Like I said earlier, Jim had unlimited powers in the state of Oregon. He went up as high as the supreme court. I think he could have gotten a governor elected anytime he wanted to. At that time he was very much in demand in other cities. He didn't move out of Portland but other cities had requested that he go up there and take them over. This was because he was runnning the situation in Portland so smoothly; there was no trouble, no difficulty at anytime. It just ran like clockwork. He was a very capable organizer. He was cold-blooded too. Nothing got in his road that he couldn't take care of. He had no fear of anything.

He had originally done time on a life sentence in Arizona. He got a fix and got out of it. He had a lifetime parole that he stay out of the state. Then he got that fixed so that he could go down there anytime he wanted. We went down there a lot of times to Tempe, Arizona, where his home was.

Many years later, after I had left Jim, the Teamsters decided to take over in Portland. Jim knew what they were doing, but they didn't think he knew. They got the mayor and a couple of the city councilmen on their side. They were going to run him out of town and run the business themselves. They all underestimated Jim. He went and rented two apartments right next to one another. In one of the apartments he put a tape recorder and in the other one he bugged every room. He had an expert do it for him. Everytime one of these fools would come down there to visit with the local Teamsters he would tell this other guy to use his empty apartment instead of staying in a hotel. Hold your meetings up there; he didn't care. They would go up there and look around a little bit. They weren't quite sure what they were looking for. So consequently, they didn't find anything. They would hold their meetings. In the next apartment was a guy hired by Jim to sit there and run the tape recorders. After they had their meeting, the guy would take the tape off and take it out to Jim's house. I listened to a few of the tapes and they would flat make this statement: "As soon as we acquire this we will get rid of that Jim." So he was forewarned everytime and could move ahead of them. They couldn't understand that. Finally, it came to a head and blew up. There was a Senate investigation at that time going on around the U.S. and they picked Portland as one of the places to hold it.

Jim asked me to come back and help him, which I did. I went to Washington D.C. with Jim and I met Bob and John Kennedy. I saw Hoffa there, who was a pretty tough young guy at that time. He was very capable of the job he inherited from Dave Beck. I knew Dave Beck here in Seattle. After these hearings Jim lost Portland and could never get it back.

I remember an incident that happened in Portland one time. Two guys that were more or less affiliated with us (they were gunmen) were arrested in a car with pistols. They were locked up and they got word to Jim. The next day Jim had made an appointment with the captain of that shift to talk to him to get these guys sprung. They were held on an open charge. Since Jim had another appointment, he told me to go down to the captain and find how much it will cost to square these guys up. I went down to the appointment place. When the captain drove up in his car I walked over and got into his car. I asked how much it would cost to spring the guys. He got very indignant and told me to get out of his car and then he drove off. I went back to the office and waited for Jim to come in. He then talked to the captain on the telephone. After he hung up he said, "If I want diplomacy I'm sure not going to send you for it. If I want the truth I'll send you but as far as a diplomat, you are the worst."

I knew that the captain was on our payroll and I knew that he had been doing business with us. So I couldn't see any sense in wasting time talking to him for a half an hour. I wasn't very enthusiastic about talking to him anyhow. In the old days he had given me a couple of dumpings so I had no love for him.

Jim was a diplomat; believe me he was a natural psychologist. He could charm the rattlers off of a rattlesnake. He charmed me for many years.

At the time that he was the boss of the town and the head of the local syndicate they wouldn't even advance an officer to captain without his OK. In fact when the chief who had been on for a long time retired, Jim had his own appointed. He had this man completely under his domination.

Making the payoffs was done in two or three different ways. In the higher echelons they were a little bit more careful. In the lower echelons detectives merely came up to the office where we had all the slot machines stored and got their payoff.

In the East the syndicate is in the rackets. See, there's a distinction. Prostitution is rackets. Gambling is rackets. Narcotics is rackets. You call it a crime because it's a violation of the law but it's—we call it— the racket. Where a thief is a stickup man, box man, a check-thief, like that. The guys that went into the syndicates were the same guys that bootlegged. That's how they got started. See, they went from stealing to bootlegging and then they went into the syndicates. The syndicates run out around Kansas City and then they begin to taper off. Colorado, Wyoming, you know, Utah, they don't have any syndicates to speak of. Then your syndicate will run down into Nevada; they control Las Vegas and the majority of gambling joints.

If you're working for the syndicate, it's pretty hard to get out of it once you get into it. They'll worry about it and then life is so cheap that they'd as soon dump you and get rid of you rather than monkey around with you. Life is cheap because these guys come out of the ghettos, I guess you call them. Real poor people in the East who live in those slums. One time, I don't recall what district it was but it was real poor, I went up to get this girl who was visiting her folks. She'd asked me to pick her up. She was a thief girl, you know, and she was an outright thief girl, not a prostitute. And I went up to this place and there was a walk, boy, and it stunk terribly when I went in. I went up on the floor and I guess offhand, I didn't count them, there was about six apartments in there. No more than two-room apartments. All these people living there and there was one toilet at the end of the hall for all these apartments and it didn't even have a door on it. Well, when you got little kids growing up that way, well, they got to think like the thieves they eventually will be. They lose all principles and morals and everything else in that. So when those guys grow up they steal milk bottles.

A thief cannot go in the rackets; a buck don't mean nothing to him. It's real hard for a thief to plan, what you call, by the month. If I got a buck in my pocket then I spend the buck. If I ain't got it then I look around for one. You're trained that way for years so to become adjusted to working the rackets is very hard for you. That's why we go broke. A businessman would say, "Well, I can't do this." We'd close the shop down and invest $100,000 in remodeling. The business didn't warrant it, but we like the fancy joint. See, we invested $100,000, we'll just say, to make the joint real fancy and we ain't got a chance to get that out in ten years. But we'd do it anyhow. Where a businessman wouldn't do that. He'd say, "Well, the joint takes in so much; we'll spend $5,000, you know; next year we'll spend another $5,000." I went broke in several businesses that way.

A thief cannot become a successful businessman. On the average, he can't. He hasn't got a chance. He has got to stay in his own business. That's why the syndicates are still staying in the rackets. They spend money getting into these legitimate businesses they hardly don't make no money in.

The rackets are run just like any other business. Of course there is a lot of conniving. They—the board—will vote to who is to be president: well they pretty near always try to pick the smartest guy in the syndicate when one of them dies. It's just like an airplane company. One guy's in hydroplane or hydrofoil or whatever they're working on now; another board member has another department. Well, it's the same when one of the board members owns gambling, one prostitution, like that. That's up to him to make that department pay. There is no difference. It's the same as a legitimate business, I'd say.

Legitimate businesses are working in the rackets. They get the fix in and they get double-crossed in it, like Boeing. They get double-crossed when MacNamara—when the TFX Contract, or whatever it was, went to Texas. Well, they can have the same thing happen in the police department. They get some inspector or something that is a square-john and he is going to raid everything that is illegal. And he can really shake them up sometimes. But they take care of it before it's over with. So does Boeing; it will overcome this DPX.

Syndicates are just as legitimate as far as operation as any other business is. That's the way they operate. Everything is done in a business-like way. Killing people is quite common in the East. If you knew an individual and he was suddenly missed from his neighborhood, you have a choice of thinking that he's takin' off—come out to the West Coast, which isn't very good thinking—or been iced, which is more likely.

5

The Thief's World

"Professional theft is just like the rest of the world: kind of falling apart."

There are about four or five thieves that are considered to have any class at all. We don't consider car theft and things like that as professional theft. There are guys who do it for a living and make a very good living from it because there are some states in the East and middle states where you can drop a car without any bill of sale, registration or anything.

A stickup man isn't so high class a thief anymore. It's become pretty low class. A safe man is supposed to be pretty high class. A safe man is rated as the top and the con man, I would say, is second. A stickup man comes third. There aren't too many con men around anymore; that's another business that went over to the women. Women are considered almost exclusively now. The pigeon drop that you read about occasionally in the paper, it is always women that do it. It used to be two men and a woman; now it's all women.

The shoplifter is about the lowest. Most of them steal through necessity; they're eatin' goofballs, shootin' dope or somethin' like that so that they do it as matter of supporting the habit, not because it's a lucrative trade—it isn't.

Then.there are some new kinds of thieves—I just watched one of them here about six weeks ago. I walked into a supermarket and watched a girl beatin' the till. She just turned the cashier around. She gave the cashier an argument, "I gave you a ten dollar bill," and she reaches over the till and gets the girl turned around by saying, "Is that fellow the manager? I want to talk to him," and when the girl turned her head—bang—she had the paper [money] out of the drawer. Just turned around and said, "I'll see the manager later," and walked out. That's all there was to it.

And there are meter-beaters. They're the guys who go around here beatin' these parking meters. Most of them get a key made. The key is fairly easy to make. They have a new key that's made by an electronic engineer here, a legitimate businessman, and they can change the key now so that it will fit any meter. The kids used to carry a ring of keys when they opened these meters. Now they have one that by just changin' a little dial on it they can use one key and open any meter in any district. We call those kind of thieves "boot and shoe thieves." Where that's derived from is when they start stealing with a boot on one foot and a shoe on the other.

One type of theft that you don't have out here [in the West] is pickpockets. They are very clever. And they stay in their own field and don't mix with anyone hardly. But in the East there are a lot of 'em. Chicago, New York and places like that. Subways and stuff like that is where they work best. Women make good boosters [shoplifters]. They are better than men. They got more places to hide the stuff than a man has.

Gamblers, prostitutes and drug peddlers aren't considered thieves. They're a breed of their own. I mean, we consider them rackets, not thieves. Gamblers and prostitutes mix together; a large percentage of the gamblers are pimps. I don't think that any one of the three in the gambling field is in the stealing field.

Among thieves, stickup men and box men are the only two that mix together. They're two different breeds—a safe man very seldom carries a gun and will never commit a stickup. I had a partner one time, a personal friend that was a stickup man; I tried time after time to get him to go with me on a box job; he just wouldn't go. He was scared to death. But he'd walk into a supermarket where there were twenty people and stick it up, and I'd be scared to death just standing and watching him. They hang out in their own places and they run together and know where one another is.

Even today, I been on parole for five years and even today guys still know where to find me and look me up, but it's just box men that look me up. Even today, once in a while a guy will stop by, and he wants something. He wants some information, or he wants to know where to find someone. And for some reason or other, thieves seem to always know where other thieves are. Usually they're in the penitentiary.

If a box man comes into town, if he was a good friend of mine or at one time or another he was a partner of mine, he'd just look me up for old time's sake or to see if I needed anything, or he might want a score. He might be short of money and knows if I'm on parole, that I'm not doing nothing usually. He'd look me up to see if I knew of a score. Because it's like lookin' at the girls. Whether you're going to get there or not, you're going to look and whether you're going to steal or not, you're going to look. And you automatically will case the place out. After you've been a thief for a long time, you walk in any joint. Just today I was waitin' over by Guthrie Hall [University of Washington] and nothing to do so I wandered around the place and never found a place so fat and easy, open windows and everything. I mean, it's just automatic. I didn't have anything to do so I just wandered around there looking, even though I haven't bothered anything for a long time now.

On the East Coast, gambling, prostitution and drugs are controlled by the syndicate, pretty near. It's almost impossible to work any length of time in the East without the help of the syndicate, so you become involved with the syndicate. On the West Coast there is no syndicate outside of Los Angeles and that's up and down; it's never been real solid down there. And in the Northwest they have tried time and again to move in and tie that area up—Portland, Seattle—and they finally go home and say, "Them dumb bastards should go back East so they can operate." But they can't get a toe-hold in the Northwest. Gamblers are syndicated in the respect that to go from one job to another, you have to keep your nose clean and have a pretty good reputation, like in Nevada—the syndicate has taken that over too.

Drug addiction, why, that means nothing; they just go where there is a connection and where they can make money enough to support that habit. Prostitution is the same way; it's not a syndicate but if they get a bad reputation, if they work past the landladies then they can't get in another joint. It's not a syndicate. We just don't have syndicates out here, on the West Coast. But it's all syndicate from New York to about Kansas City.

A friend of mine works for a syndicate; he's a box man; he works for the syndicate in [Kansas City]. He tried to get me to go to work for them the last time I saw him several years ago. But I couldn't see it. They send them out and knock off a box; they tell them to go get that box and might be $100,000 in it. He has to bring the money back and give it to them. If they feel like it they hand him $100. You better bring it back, too. Some people like the security, I suppose.

I talked to him quite a bit about it and tried to find out from him—feel him out—because he was a pretty capable box man. And I asked him if he didn't want to come take a tour with me on the West Coast and he said, "No, I like it here." They get in the organization and settle down. He's got a hustling girl and the syndicate takes care of it that she has a steady job. And they send him out once in a while to knock off a box and they don't have him on a salary but they take care of him. It is almost the same as a salary.

He just settles down in that group and stays there. Then, too, they've got the fix real solid in those towns. He'll never go to the penitentiary; that may have a bearing on it; he may be afraid to go to the joint. They won't go to the joint; they won't get indicted. If they get indicted, they'll get paroled off the bench and if paroled, they don't have to bother with it. They get a suspended sentence or something of that order or the case will be thrown out of court for lack of evidence or things like that. The syndicate takes care of it. They have those ward bosses back there, I believe they call them; he has a district and he takes care of it. He usually has political influence with a small politician and if need be they'll go to the boss of the syndicate and he'll take care of the big guy. He's usually got something on him—indiscretion. If necessary, if the beef [the crime] is big enough and hot enough, if it's a murder or something like that involved, then they have to pay somebody off. The judge usually gets involved. I mean this generally now, not personally. There are exceptions to this and all rules. It's usually divided between the district attorney and the judge.

If I went East and worked and got picked up by the bulls, I'd go to the joint. The district attorney has to have so many convictions; he's almost elected on the amount of convictions that he has. And somebody has to furnish them—as a stranger, I'd furnish it. But if I'm picked up on the West Coast I'd be on my own then. The thing to do then is get a good criminal attorney; there's one in every town that is usually the fix—he'll get to somebody. It will never go to a jury; I made that mistake one time, using a criminal attorney to go to a jury; I coulda done better by myself.

The fix usually knows all the connections from people on up to the top. Usually, he's a friend of one of the district attorneys, assistant district attorney or someone who can get to the district attorney. And he'll offer the district attorney whatever is necessary. Usually, the criminal attorney wants to keep it all so he'll try to use friendship or whatever means he can to persuade them to be lenient with you or let you go without having to turn loose of any of that money.

In the East they have what they call the bag man; in fact there's that in any town. The police department will designate one guy that they hope is honest and won't swing with all the money. And he goes around every month and picks up all the bribes. Different joints pay off different amounts. Any town that is running gambling—and they all do—has a bag man.

Portland had quite an accident about a year ago. The town had been closed down for a while due to a grand jury hearing but they decided to open the town up. They sent their bag man out on the first of the month and he made the collections. The town wasn't settled down enough yet for everybody to recognize this bag man so the next month when the bag man started out, well say on the third of the month, to make his collections, somebody had already made them on the first of the month. That's a dirty thief for ya.

A syndicate is a large organization. It has to be. They have a great many employees and they have an enormous payoff. A terrific payoff. The syndicates in the West are local syndicates, strictly local. They don't extend beyond the city limits of the town. The larger syndicates that I have reference to control states in the East. They send girls from one state to the other and stuff like that; you know, from one joint to another. And they own maybe three, four hundred whorehouses alone. No man on the Pacific Coast owns more than two. The pattern just isn't there. You don't have any really large syndicates out here. Don't ask me why, I don't know. But in the West they have tried to bring syndicates in and they just won't work. Them guys have really gone home talking to themselves, back to Minneapolis, you know, Kansas City and Chicago. They used to come out of Kansas City and out of Minneapolis from syndicates there, and they tried to tie up the West Coast and they just couldn't do it.

In the East, they hijack truck and trailer loads of clothing, whiskey and stuff like that. Here, I know, I drove a truck for a long time before I had a heart attack, and we've left a big semi loaded with whiskey, which is quite a large sum, sit overnight right there at the dock. No watchman or nothin'. And nobody touched it because there's no place to drop it. You have to have a syndicate, you know, involved before you could drop such a thing and there is no such thing here. The Eastern syndicate tried to take over Los Angeles but it just don't work. They go up and down there but that's all.

The syndicates have no morals, no principles or anything because back there they'll dump you in the river real easy. They get a guy, he could take over one of these towns here, I believe; it's never been done but he could, I believe. By getting real tough and dumpin' a few people in the crick and they all begin to get in line for him. And then he'd pick up three or four of the tough guys and they'd start working together—

there's the nucleus of your syndicate. Then automatically people will cater to them, enforcement people, the law and all branches—that's how they get involved with them; they seek the syndicates out. A syndicate doesn't particularly have to seek them out; it's pitiful to say, but the law will contact a syndicate through a criminal attorney or something like that and say they'll do business.

Most thieves are crossroaders—they travel around so they can't have a family. I got a friend of mine that's married and got six kids over in Ohio. I never knew he stayed home long enough to get six kids, but evidently he does or he's got a hell of a friend, I don't know which. He is married but the average guy, you see, doesn't associate with square-john broads. I mean there's too much explaining to do to a square-john broad.

Just take you and I together here for instance. You get acquainted with me someplace and like me so we go out to dinner or something together and I have to keep avoiding you. See, just little tiny normal questions that you would ask another guy without any thought and he would answer without any thought. But I have to cover up so I have to continuously stay on my toes and I can't enjoy a square-john's company—even if it's congenial company. Because you're going to ask me some questions that's going to give you a clue; afterwards you're going to think, "Well, that's an odd answer he gave me for that."

A thief thinks square-johns are crazy. See, I'd say it's crazy to get up and go to school everyday; you go in there and see the same professor and you go along like that and I'd say, "Man, let's do something else." So we both have a different point of view. When I was stealing, why I lived a lie. You automatically—what's the word—acclimate yourself to it and then you just go ahead and live it. I mean you enjoy it and get some guy in the bar and you're sittin' there and you lay an awful story on the guy and he's sittin' there shaking his head like a nut on the end of a string, you know, and he's buying the story. You get up and go on home and you say, "Why, I had an enjoyable evening."

I quite often would buy a house, you know; I've had more houses than most people buy all their life. I'd make a payment on them and live there for a little while and say to hell with it and go on. You don't pay no income tax or nothin'. What do you care? You don't care. That's the way thieves live.

I talked to quite a few kids—fourteen, fifteen, sixteen years old, just starting out—and I'd hate like hell to give them a $10 bill to take home and count out, I'll tell you. There is a lot of difference in the

thieves today than when I started and it wasn't because yesterday
things were better in every way. I just watch and I see it. I saw it the
last time I did time. The kids'd steal cigarettes from one another in the
penitentiary, beat one another, even their friends, out of things and
they are altogether different in their principles and thought. When I
was stealing, I'd talk to some other box man or a friend of mine and
I'd tell him, "Gee, I got a good caper in Seattle. If you go through there
take a look at it for me, will you, and see if you get any ideas?" He'd
look at it and find a means of entry or something important to the job.
He wouldn't dream of touching it. He'd ask me if he could go with me
on it maybe but these kids today steal from one another or steal one
another's capers or anything else, they don't care—just get that
money that's all. Then nine-tenths of the kids today are users of narcotics or goofballs or somethin'. I would say that a very small percentage of box men in my time used narcotics. You just didn't trust a guy, I
mean, who is liable to get sick because he didn't make any connection,
because he didn't have any stuff so he couldn't show up or anything.

You have to run stealing just as legitimate as you would a legitimate
business. You've got it all laid out that the bull goes by at a certain
time and you've got to be ready to go, and you can't trust a hype [a
narcotics user]. He might get sick or take an overdose or somethin'—
or just go to sleep. So that's one of the reasons we don't use one of
those guys—very unreliable.

These kids today use narcotics, chippy way; they can't afford a
habit 'cause they can't make enough money. In their capers, I mean,
they go up against $15, $20 scores—you see it in the papers every
night—these kids sticking up Ma and Pa grocery stores for $5, $10.
They go to the penitentiary for twenty years for that. And if they happen to be a little hot in town right then, they're just going to grab the
first guy that comes in and indict him and slam him in there and make
big headlines and send that guy to the penitentiary for twenty years.
We won't really argue the point whether it's right or wrong but they
will. And for a lousy $15 or $20. These kids go for them all the time
now.

When I was younger, if you put the finger on your partner why they
better lock you up way over someplace 'cause he was going to tear
your head off, if they put you in stir together. They wouldn't under
any circumstances ever let the two of you close to one another. In
fact, they tried very much to keep you separated when they sent you
to the joint, if they had to send you both up. But both of these FBI

agents and these couple of policemen I know told me that today these kids that get pinched run down and the first thing they do is make a voluntary statement involving everybody that they know. They take 'em up and lock 'em up in the same tank—they sleep together in the same cell. They don't think nothin' of it.

A stool pigeon is a dirty word with us. You just didn't do it, that's all. In all the years I stole, I only signed one statement. I was in California when I was a kid and I tried to take my partner off the hook so I signed a statement saying he had nothin' to do with it and they went in the other room and talked to him and he signed a statement saying that I had nothing to do with it. We both went to the joint. I said, "Well, this is real stupid, I'll never do this again." And I never have; I've never signed another statement, irrespective. But these kids do, they sign them right and left. They think nothin' of it. They expect it, I guess, I don't know. Professional theft is just like the rest of the world actually, kind of falling apart.

Instead of beating it out of you like when I was a kid—why you knew you was going to get a shellacking every time they'd catch you— today it's a little different; they don't shellack these guys like that. Oh, they still do it once in a while when they get a little unhappy about something, but not like they used to.

The bulls are tougher to get around today; they work together in these things. It used to be that one guy had his connections, his stool pigeons, and until he solved the case he wouldn't cooperate with nobody. But this going to FBI school has taught the cops a lot of things. They now make out a report, their thoughts about it and what they saw, and turn it in and the lieutenant or captain will give it to the next shift, and they go right on. It's not a personal affair no more like it used to be. That makes it tough for the thief because he had terrific odds against him to start with, even in the old days.

I got this book to read the other day; *The Professional Thief.** Basically I heartily agree with what the con man says; small things that he says in there I disagreed with. He uses different categories altogether of the thief we know. He uses Eddie Garron; I know him personally. He wrote books. He's full of bull. Ernie Booth wrote a lot of books; he just wrote them to make money; there's no truth to it. You know, he takes a little bit of truth and makes a big story out of it and sells the

---

*Edwin H. Sutherland, *The Professional Thief* (Chicago: University of Chicago Press, 1937).

book. And Black Jack; Black Jack was a Boston thief, and I knew him when he was on the coast one time; he was an old-timer. Ernie Booth was a stickup man and bank robber at that time and Eddie Garron, he escaped from Devil's Island and went to Paris and held up the American Railway Express there, which at that time was the medium of exchange, you know, all over the world for Americans to change money. Eddie Garron tried it out, and they got a terrific sum of money but they got caught before they could get out of there. They have an Interpol over there. That's a smart police force, smarter than the FBI even.

This guy in *The Professional Thief* doesn't really cover the different types of professional thieves. Of course, it's a small book; I read it in a couple of hours. It's real easy. He leaves out the different categories of thieves that he's not acquainted with. Confidence men and stuff like that are in a class of their own; we don't want a man to have anything to do with them. They are a smooth, fancy-dressed thief and I've only known one or two in my life; I've never known any others. And that's what he was, a con man.

And he was in the days of the pickpocket, while today pickpocketing is over almost. There are very few pickpockets around now; especially on the West Coast there are hardly any. And what few there are usually are girls. The funny part is that these girls don't appear to have any ability on their own, no initiative I guess, to do something; somebody will turn them out and make a whore out of them, and they'll put them to work as a pickpocket, and they turn out to be the greatest, but girls won't do it learning by themselves. And like at the World's Fair, why when the fair was on here in Seattle, there were a couple of crews working and they were all women and just one or two guys. Of all the people and thieves I know, I only know one pickpocket and he's young, and it just happens that he's a natural, you know. The pickpocket is kind of an outlaw of his own.

This guy makes a big issue out of a booster [shoplifter], and a booster is the lowest class thief there is. You know, a shoplifter; kids shoplift and so do old broken-down housewives and these guys that eat dope and yellowjackets all the time. There's nothing high class about a shoplifter. Hell, they're the lowest there is, and he's putting them in with the con man, you know, mixing them together. Even in his time, why they had no class. He's confused on it, on that issue there. He did a lot of research work, and used other guys' stuff, which he admits, well he has to; I recognized a little bit of Eddie Garron in there. I can't remember what Eddie Garron wrote now. But he used some of

Ernie Booth, who is quite a writer and quite a talker, you know, and I would say efficient writer, *We Robbed a Bank,* and things like that. I remember some of the titles, but I forget all about these guys. It's been so many years.

A booster is just about the lowest thief there is. Nobody has much to do with them. I mean I seen one yesterday; as a matter of fact, I saw this one, then talked to this other guy who was a meter-robber, you know, a guy who robs parking meters. They make a lot of money. I was talking to this friend and he said he saw Charlie Jay boosting the other day. I told him, "Gee, Charlie Jay. Man, I can remember when he was a real high-class thief." "Oh," he said, "he's down at the bottom now." In our estimation he's down dragging bottom because he's boosting. And he used to be a real high-class thief at one time.

At one time box men were rated as the kings, but then there weren't so many kids to rip it and tear, now it's lost its good name. Bank robbers used to be a high-class profession, but all these kids around robbing them now ain't getting nothing out of them. They used to get $100,000 to $200,000 out of a bank; now they get $3,000 or $4,000. So that profession fell down to the bottom. A good safe man is still rated as up in the upper categories. A con man is right on the top. I've watched them work and I've got the utmost respect for their ability, but as I said they're kind of separated from the rest of the thieves. And they enjoy it, I mean, taking some Hoosier and turning him around.

They all pay off; all con men pay off. You read the paper where someone got beat here; well they make a big issue of it, then the bulls get paid off, the "Bunco" squad they call it.

Stickup man. I'm against it, see, so I'm prejudiced. I think that a great many of the thieves here don't like stickup men because he puts a lot of fire on the other thieves. So I'm not particularly enthused about them. They are more of an outlaw.

Then today there are new types of thief. Two guys will go in the store and get in two different lines. One of them will wait until the cashier has opened the register and start a big fuss about the bill or somethin', then the guy in the other line reaches his hand over and takes a handful of bills. It's real simple. They just grab it and walk out. We call these guys till-tappers.

There's other rackets that make good money. I know guys that have stolen trucks and sold them and make good money on it. And they have no rating at all because it's something that isn't done very often.

Not on the West Coast. On the East Coast you've got a lot of it; right down in Virginia, West Virginia, in that area, there's three or four rings operating all the time. Out here on the West Coast we don't have much of that.

A guy came to me with a government check for $3,700.00 a while back and wanted me to take it. Well, I explained it to him; I know the guy well so that I could tell him so he'd understand it. See, the check was an income tax check that was delivered to the wrong address, and they went to a great deal of trouble to hunt the guy and get his signature and everything. And he wanted me to get rid of the check. But they wanted $3,000 for their end. I told them you ain't got nothing. When I'm operating, a guy finds a mark for me, I don't give a darn if it's a $100,000 mark, he gets ten percent. He gets it if it's only a $1,000 mark, "but you guys ain't got nothing—you've just got the check." I said they can go out to our mailboxes and get a thousand checks, and they ought to take ten percent or whatever they want to give you because the check is going to go from here down to Nevada where it will be cashed, run in a gambling joint. Then the gambling joint gets a piece of the action; the guy that took the check down there will get a piece of the action, and by the time they get through cutting it up, they're lucky if they get anything themselves. That check is liable to run clear into Mexico before it reaches the money. You ain't got nothing there. They seemed to think they have. You know, all the time they don't understand. I would no more send that guy down there than fly a kite.

This guy that I was talking to yesterday, now he's got some good connections in Reno. Well, I wouldn't even dream of asking him. If I had some hot stones (diamonds or other precious gems) or something, I say, "Gerry, can you get rid of these?" And I'd cut him in for a piece of the action before I'd gotten him to get rid of them for me. But on the East you can go into the syndicates and places like that if you can get in, if you're strong enough. It's pretty hard for a stranger, but if you're strong enough to stand the opposition you can. I can go into Kansas City or Toledo and I've got some connections there. I'd have to hunt around, and it would take me two or three weeks to do it—I could talk them into taking these stones but they wouldn't take them themselves. They would have a fence someplace in Chicago or New York or someplace, and they would say, go and see the guy and call me.

See, you don't have that here, but when I was young, there was such a thing on the West Coast. I know there were fences all up and down. There was a big one in Seattle, there was a big one in San Francisco, there was a big one in Los Angeles. And the guys could trust one another, but you can't trust anybody anymore—they'll all tell.

Paper laying [writing bad checks] today is done by the majority of thieves. When I was stealing, in fact, we would just leave money orders and checks in the safe; we wouldn't touch them. All we took was the cash or gold, or narcotics, or something like that. If we found jewelry we would look it over very carefully and pry the stones out and throw the rings away. The gold has no value in a ring, you know. Nowadays, they steal the money orders. And they put them down and let them lay for a year, and they'll cash them themselves. In my time we didn't do that.

These paper hangers—that's a disease, believe me. They have no control over themselves. I worked for a guy down here on Second Avenue and Senca tending bar and a couple of guys that was in Walla Walla* when I was there walked right in there and tried to hand me a personal check. They were dead serious, trying to hand me a personal check. And I was standing talking to them a few minutes before and they'd say, "Well I'm working now and everything and will you cash a personal check?" I know it's bum paper when they hand it to me and laugh and tear it in two and tell him, "You're sure a Simple Simon if I've ever seen one, trying to turn a paper on me; get out of here." They can't help it. They don't stop and think whether they're going to win or not, you know; they're just going to lay it all over town and they know that the check squad's going to get them. See, they've got no chance to beat them; their handwriting's on the check.

There's a guy that comes through here that has a good racket; he has someone else endorse these money orders and he covers up real good when he goes in and cashes them. Why, he'll talk to you and keep you moving around until he gets you off balance and then he'll pretend he's endorsing the check and hand it to you. And he hasn't done anything; he's using a ball point pen without any ink in it. And he covers it up. He's pretty clever at it. Consequently, there is no signature in his handwriting on there at all. But that's the exception. The average paper layer, they go out and steal these payroll checks and they cash them with their fingers crossed, you know, hoping they can lay them. It's in the papers and everyone looks out for them, all over our area. They stole some from the P.I., the [Seattle] newspaper, and then

---

*The maximum security Washington State penitentiary.

laid one in the next block, at Denny's, $120 I think it was; and Denny
and everybody else knew the checks was no good, but they waited till
payday, see, and when the P.I. got paid, why they just moved in very
quick with their checks and waited. Personally, I can't see it, but
that's their racket. $120 ain't much money.

Counterfeiting is a one-man operation. It's widespread when it goes
down—this one guy, I don't know who he is but he makes real good
paper, real good, and I know two or three crews that would go and
buy it from back East. Well, he just mixes up a batch of it and puts it
away, you know, and then peddles it to all them guys and they circulate it to all these gambling joints: the best of the paper. And they'll go
in and buy a short stack of chits; then they'll go to the table and they'll
start betting cash; they'll buy chits right there at the table with cash
and they'll use up the money that way to cash it in, and they're going
to the pocket all the time with these chits, you know. They're just laying down the losers in cash. They also work these supermarkets in the
busiest part of the day. In the evening, you know, they'll work in
there—they always work in crews, men and women together. Usually, thieves and whores will do that.

A good counterfeiter—there is no such thing. Uncle Sam nails them.
I saw one of them bills they had here a while back, that they were fin-
ished with, and believe me, it was a perfect bill. There was only one
tiny mark on it, one real tiny mark on it that identified it. Even banks
took them at first, you know. This one guy, he spoiled it here because
he got caught with it. But they laid a lot of it. You know, when stuff
like that comes up, that scares them 'cause they know that most of
them guys come from the East, those guys that do that work. So they
know that that paper could come all the way from here to New York,
you know, in the process of being turned loose. Especially when they
go into Mexico, they go to Tijuana to the track or something like that.
They're going to send that money back, and Uncle's got to catch up
with you. If they find you with a counterfeit bill they just take it away
from you and give you a receipt. You never get any money for it. But if
a foreign country turns that money in, they want money and they get it
from us. You know they don't want any fuss with them so they pay
them off.

Anybody can lay phony money. I mean you could walk in and hand
it to the guy and be ready to run if he shows any indication. But they
call their shots, you know, and get a busy bar, get a beer, lay down a
$20 bill. Usually, then they will whip to the next bar. Anyone can do it.

Kids can do it. In fact, young girls are the best at it. You know, the bartender is looking at the girl instead of the $20 bill. So they're not very high up the ladder. They serve another clan of some kind, and they've just had a chance to buy up a lot of that money, and they're laying it.

The rackets are very mixed today. When I was learning to be a box man, I didn't do nothing but box work, absolutely nothing; the stickup man never did anything but stickups. Now, why, they mix all over, you know, they do anything. I think that I was a forerunner of mixing up rackets. I found one time that I had terrific amount of heat on me. Copper and brass was worth its weight in gold at that time, so I just started looking around for wholesale places; I was looking for a whole truckload. I could drive semi, so we would go steal a semi on a weekend, which would be laid up and wouldn't be used much. In fact we would usually take it back and then find a fence. All junk men are fences and we would just peddle the whole thing, you know, and then get $8,000 to $10,000 for the whole load; copper, truck and all. But most thieves stick to one racket.

It's just like this kid that opens these parking meters. He can make a key for any of them. Any of these laundromats, money-changers or anything. And he makes his own keys, see; he'll steal the lock and he makes his own keys. And I tell him, "Man get out of that, get into something else. The bulls all up and down the Coast know ya." He makes a heck of a salary, you know. He works a couple of nights and makes himself $300 or $400 but he won't change. He came up to my place here, see, and he was walking down the street, trying out a key. Making a new key, you know; they're quite complicated, the keys they use today. He can make keys for anything.

We don't have too many burglars up in this country. You take around Los Angeles, you know; they did some real high-class burglaries down there, but you East Coast is where your big burglaries are; we don't have anything to interest them out here. See, there's nothing out in this area here. This is Hoosier country, I'm not belittling it, I don't use that expression that way, but it's a Hoosier country in the respect that they lock up their furs, you know, they don't keep them home. Back East they think nothing of it.

I went in to open a safe one time for some guys and it was in a closet, and this guy takes ten pieces of fur—coats and capes or what the heck they are—down, before I could burn that box out of there. And I've never heard of such a thing on the West Coast. You see, these people just don't have 'em. Your wealthiest people will have one or two fur coats, that's all. Till you get down around that Los Angeles–Hollywood area, you know. So really, you don't have any high-class burglars up here.

Another thing is the heeler. A heeler is a hotel prowler and in my mind they're the greatest. I went around with a heeler one time and he just shook me to pieces when he'd go in there and reach under people's pillows while they're sleeping and steal their wallet. He went from hotel prowling to motel prowling. See, they stay in motels now. So they go into that and you'd be dumbfounded to know the people who leave the door open. You'd just be dumbfounded. Successful businessmen. Course I've always said that I can't condemn a thief because of the stupid things the legitimate people do. They go out for the evening, they leave their front door unlocked. So you'll be sure to be able to get in. They beg for it, you know, leave their front porch light on and leave the front door unlocked and stuff like that. Hotel prowling is an old business, but motel prowling is new but it would come in the same category, so that wouldn't be new. Parking meters and till-tapping—they're new.

They used to heel on boxes. Boxes would be on what they call "day com." A man would come in and open the safe in the morning and take a certain amount of money out. He wanted to leave the bulk in there and then he'd turn the safe to one number. He didn't want to go all through that process if he had to go into the safe again. The box is usually in the back room or in the office or something so these heelers go 'round—these daytime heelers—and they go in and look around and they find one of these safes and they just whip in there and try what you call the mit, and if the door didn't open they can turn it one number each way and try it and nine times out of ten they'd open it and get the money out. They call them "daytime heelers."

Today, the majority of thieves are hypes. They'd shoot anything—any narcotic—they don't know what it means to really be a hype. They shoot anything and think they're getting a charge out of it. It's just like prohibition. The quicker they take us and turn us loose and let them go in the drugstore and buy it the quicker they are going to get straightened around.

The language of thieves has changed. Today they got a couple of new languages. Guys have talked to me about it—talked to me in it. We would be eating—I'd take them over to dinner with me when they'd talk in it, these younger ones—and I couldn't understand it. See, it's a new language. They've always had a language. The terms that they used would lap over from juvenile delinquency; maybe that was always so—I don't know. It might have been so when I was young, when it was brought over from juvenile delinquency. Some of the terms were used in the 1800s in England and France. I think that we have something that was built three and four hundred years back. You know, our language and just a word here and there added to it. But today these kids and their jive talk is all different.

I served three years apprenticeship, man. Today these kids—somebody shows them how to hot-wire a car and they're a thief. See, they're gone right then.

We have a lot of terms we use that will allow you to talk in front of somebody. Just the terms in themselves will let you talk in front of somebody. And they can't pick up on it. You have to be extremely careful because they think there's something wrong with you if you get to using it on some waitress or something like that. I took a fellow over to eat a while back and he used a lot of those terms that I could pick up on. Just terms in a conversation, and the waitress would look at him like he got rocks in his head, you know, and I told him, "The broad is giving you a rank here man; you better lay off." That's an illustration, you know. You're getting a rank from the broad; they know what the word broad means but they don't usually pick up on it. Because a man don't use the expression in front of a woman. A thief will; they call all women broads.

I took two kids under my wing when I was rootin' the last time and I tried to teach them. I'd take them to San Francisco after we made two or three scores up in this country and they was terrible. I took them in up on Powell, someplace there. I try the joint and told them I'm going to get a suit. So, I take them in there and this guy asked them, "What price would you like to go?" Before I could step in, you know, why they're stumbling around there with their conversation until the guy ranked that something was wrong with them. And I told him, "Well, $250 or somewheres in that neighborhood." We had the money and I wanted them to look good. I think they slept in the damn suits, to tell you the truth. They embarrassed me so much.

When I'm stealing, I'm always eating at the best places. I enjoyed the food, but mainly it's because policemen never go to the best places. They can't. So that's the best place to go and eat. If you want to drink, go the to best cocktail lounge in town. There won't be no bulls there. So you avoid any heat. That's why I never mix with these guys in these other joints.

Thieves have attachments every place. If I have some stuff to sell I can't drop it with a fence in the East unless I know somebody. Well, I know a guy that works for a syndicate in Kansas City. One other guy I know don't work for the syndicate no more but is connected with it because he used to and the fence would accept his word. He lives in Cleveland. I'd just go to him and tell him, "Hey, Pete, I got some ice here I want to dump. You can make a few bucks, if you want." That's all. That's why these thieves come see me all the time. I don't want them to see me. I got nothing to talk over with them anymore. But they find out where you're at. I don't care where you're at. They'll find it out. See, you can't get away from it; there's no way. You'd be surprised at the population of ex-cons–ex-thieves all around the country.

There is no loyalty among thieves today. There's no such thing at all. They have absolutely no loyalty. They'll beat one another to the money, you know, anything they can; they beat one another for their girls, or anything. Thieves have brought me stuff and I've held it for two or three years and worried about it all the time for fear I'd lose it. Because I could hardly face the guy if I'd lost it even if he wouldn't believe that I'd sold it or anything; I'd be so ashamed.

Some guy would ask, "What do you think you could get for this, Harry?" Maybe I'd go to a fence for him and try to dump it if he was a stranger, you know; I'd try to dump it for him and the fence would say, "Well, I'll give you so much." And I'd tell the guy to bring it up or wherever he had it and I'd give it to the fence and the fence would say, "I don't think it's worth that much now." Well, I've taken money out of my pocket to make up the difference with the guy, because I just didn't want the guy to think that I may be chiseling on him or something. Even though he wouldn't think it, I don't think.

If you had any class as a thief in an area you could go on the cuff. Partners would take up a collection to send a guy money in the joint or something but they would never take up a collection among thieves who weren't his partners. They're not quite that bighearted.

Thieves in the East work approximately the same as in the West, though they're much more progressive, see—all your safe companies and everything are in the East. And it's like styles in clothing. I've been East and seen a style in clothing; come back out here and six months later we get it. Well, the same way thieves will learn about safes. They need to know angles on how to beat a new box.

One time two guys out of Kansas City had been sent to me and they had a couple of scores—one in San Francisco and one in Vancouver, B.C.—and they wanted me to go with them. They were strangers out here, and it's pretty hard to start working right away if you're not acquainted with the country. I didn't go with them but I helped them get straightened around so they could work. And they beat a round-door that I had seen but hadn't managed to find out yet how to beat. And they already knew and had been using it in the East. They knew more about that stuff long before we know about it here—long before.

In the East the syndicate uses professional thieves to steal papers. See they've gone into legitimate businesses and they want to know about some bids or something and they'll have a box man go beat that box and he'll take and read up on these papers. They tell him to and he'll make it look like he was after the money alone. He'll throw the papers all over the office, but in the meantime he's copied down the bids, you know, something of that order. Whatever they send him for. It might be some guys imported a bunch of diamonds. The syndicate heard about them and they want them so they send this box man to get them.

Maybe he won't work for a long time, and they'll give him a little piece of action around town—maybe cutting in with the landlady in some whorehouse, you know. And tell her, "Here's your new old man." You know, that's all, and he gets that and he'll go along with it. But it's not a very lucrative deal. You do what the syndicate tells you to do.

But those guys back there never had nothing to start with, see. So it's been a real tough scuffle all their life. On the West Coast, you got a lot more space to move around in. You haven't got the syndicate to contend with. You find a gambling joint out here, you knock it off, that's all. Period. Anything is yours that you can take. Back there you got to worry about the syndicates, getting in their face all the time and if they get hot they'll help the bulls catch you.

One time a friend of mine wanted to come into Portland and open up a bootleg joint. He went to the bulls and told them that he wanted to open it up and the bulls told him, "Well, all right, it will cost you so much a month but when some thief comes in and gets red hot and he's in your joint hanging around we want to know about it." Lou told 'em,

"Man, I'm no stool pigeon." They said, "Well, that's the way it is. Everybody does it so you're going to do it too." There's no honor among heads of the rackets, believe me. They'll dump anybody. Same as lawyers. This fix business ain't all it's cut up to be. They make a trade-off quite often; you see that fix is working in the district attorney's office. You know, you got to work with them and that district attorney's guys got to make so many convictions a year. Usually they'll get the conviction and then spring the guy. Or get the conviction and then sentence him to a minor sentence.

Even in the county jail, for two or three hundred you get out in a couple weeks. You pay the head jailer off out here. They've had some very embarrassing moments over that where a guy'll get pinched two or three times in a year and get a year each time. And often people have asked about it.

But the fix is just as likely to make a bargain in the district attorney's office and let's say there are three of you arrested—and he goes up there. In my case, I was putting up the bank roll because I didn't spend mine very fast where the two other guys did. Well, I fronted for us and I did the talking 'cause I'd known the fix for a long time. And, he said, "I don't know if I can get all three of you off." See, I told him now, "Man, don't pull that with me," 'cause I know what he's thinking. It's so simple for him to go to the D.A. and say, "Look, turn Harry loose and eat up the other two." I could have talked the other two into it. They'd a went for it. I'd made them a lot of money and everything. Taught 'em how to open safes. So they owed me something. But I told Abe, "All or none." You know, so we got the beef squared. Cost us a chunk of money. It costs $5,000 or $10,000 to fix them beefs.

You just read about these guys getting $147,000 in Idaho. Man, did you ever stop to think how much of that money they'll wind up with? They'll wind up with a chunk of it all right because the score was so big. The first place, offhand, there were two boxes. I know that because they've already talked to me about it. There's two boxes there, and there was doubt as to whether or not they'd blow them or peel them. But these guys have got to take into account the fact that it belongs to the government, that it's a thousand to one that those bills have been numbered in the bank where they came from, Federal Reserve or wherever—they'll all be new money. Them guys can't touch that money for a year at least—it'll be a year before they can touch it. And in the meantime, they'll be hauling it down to Nevada, or someplace, to get rid of it. And they're going to take a beating there because when they take it down there, right away those people are going to know where that money came from because that's the biggest score been made around here for quite a while. So they'll hem-haw around; they know they got these guys on the hook and they'll hem-haw around and say they don't want to monkey with that. Them guys will keep dropping down and droppin' their price, you know, until they get down, I'll betcha, from $147,000—I'll betcha they don't get $50,000 out of it.

Well, you split it up with three guys and, hell, we was making that much out of a couple Safeways, see. Plus they got Uncle crazy to find 'em. And he'll find 'em. All they got is the reputation for making $147,000. That's like the Brink's job. They wound up with nothing. They was professional thieves as I say the professional thief is in the East. They were raised in these tenements, you know, and grew up together. And had no principles, no character; that's why these guys are gettin' fingered. But the caper was so simple that they couldn't miss. They just couldn't. For they even had keys to the place to beat the doors. Oh, it was terrific, you know, it was so simple. And there was a case of putting it together—they were professional thieves all right 'cause they were committing stickups all the time, but they weren't high-class thieves by any means. There was only one guy—and he turned out to be the rottenest—that had any brains in him.

One thing I wish I knew a little bit more about—why thieves prefer whores. Whores or somebody that will sleep with guys for money. You would think that a guy wouldn't want anything to do with one of them. I don't mean necessarily for the money that they make, but thieves usually pick out whores for companions. It must be that we are on the same level or something. I know that even today, in the majority of cases, I prefer what we call a rounder girl in preference to a square-john girl. It seems like they have a better understanding or they just accept us for what we are. A square-john girl has a tendency to want to change us or make us over. Then, too, you get used to what square-johns think is an abnormal sex life.

A friend of mine married a square-john girl in Portland. If you call him up she gets all upset about it. She's afraid that he is going to get in trouble. Where a whore won't do that. She has respect for her old man. She thinks he is capable of deciding for himself whether or not he might get in trouble.

My brother was a house burglar. I am always curious as to how the other half lives. One night I went out with him. We went in this house.

I always develop a terrific thirst when I am working on the job. I will usually drink a pop or something like that. Perspiration just pours off of me. Not because I am afraid; it's just nerves I guess. While my brother was shaking this house down, I wandered out in the kitchen and there was this ice box. I thought that they would have some milk or something in there. I took ahold of the door and pulled it open and somebody turned the light on. I slammed that door so quick. I had never given it a thought that when you open a refrigerator door the light comes on in it. There I was in a cold dark house, the curtains up, these people away. I opened up this refrigerator that turned on a light that shined all over the kitchen. Believe me, it frightened me. I wasn't made for a house burglar.

I went with him one time to this house where he thought there was a safe. It was a big house in the Hollywood district. It belonged to somebody in the movie industry. There was a big patio right beside the house. It was an enormous place. A big police dog was there, which was supposed to be on patrol. My brother could charm these dogs; he could make friends with any of them. By the time we got this dog straightened around we climbed over the fence into the yard. This dog was following us around. I am walking on this white tile and I walked right into the swimming pool. I didn't even see it until I walked into it. That terminated that night because I was just like a drowned rat. We had to get in the car and go home. My brother was very unhappy that I was so stupid as to walk into the swimming pool. Supermarkets don't have swimming pools.

As I say, to each his own. That field is not for me. I never cared for it and I never want anything to do with it. Especially the way he operates. He gets in his car and drives around until he finds a house where the lights are all out. On the same night he will knock off this house. Well we don't do it that way. We usually case a place for three days at least. Sometimes a lot more than that. But he does it one way and we do it another. He can't understand this laying on a joint for several days before we knock it over. By the same token I can't understand him knocking one over the same night he discovers that there is nobody home. He gets such a small percentage for what he gets in the way of jewelry and stuff like that. He has got some paintings that were real expensive. When he peddled them he never got anything for them. Maybe just a few dollars. And I know that the paintings cost thousands of dollars, because I recognized the names of painters that were on them. If he gets two percent for jewelry he is doing pretty good.

I have talked to a lot of guys lately, safe men, who are professionals. I find that about seventy-five percent of them are carrying guns today. That is something that was very unusual in old time safe men where I was raised. So evidently the trend is changing and we have that old story again, which came first, the egg or the chicken. I don't know whether the police have become worse about shooting guys or whether the younger guys have just become tougher about that like the East Coast. On the East Coast, everybody carries a gun on a caper. This happens, I found, clear over into Montana. But around the Pacific Coast very few professional safe men used to carry a gun. And now the majority of them do. We have had two or three shootings here among safe men, where they have been shot up by policemen. I guess the trend is changing a great deal.

No matter how smart he is, every thief is going to spend time in the joint. Sometimes you just can't fix a beef. It gets a little too hot. You know, you get into town, you tear it all apart. You stay there too long and you keep rootin'. Maybe it's a good town and there's a lot of good scores in it. Well, you just keep on rooting against your better judgement. But thieves are lazy by nature and when they find so many soft touches they just keep on workin'. Well the police department gets hotter and hotter; all that adverse publicity and the insurance company puts pressure on the supermarkets and they pressure the police so when they do catch ya, they won't listen to your fix. So you have to go.

Or occasionally you get caught without any money and you're in strange country where you know you have no contacts or anything and you're going to go. One of my partners just got five years in Deer Lodge about a month ago. I just heard that he didn't have any money and he got five years out of it. If I could've gotten ahold of him or he could've gotten word to me soon enough I would have tried to help him. Most of the older thieves, if they gave their word to a bondsman that they would pay—like my bond is good to $100,000 on the Pacific Coast—he'd accept that because he knows that they'll pay it. Thieves, professionals I mean, are very reliable about paying their debts.

6

The Thief and the Law

". . . the only people that really profit from theft is the fix, the judge and the district attorney."

Frankly, after sitting down and analyzing it I come to the conclusion that the only people that really profit from theft is the fix, the judge, and the district attorney. They're the guys who make the money, not the guy who stole it. The guy who stole it is always getting pinched, and they're shaking him down for what he's got. I've had 'em flat pinch me on the street and shake me right down, take me in the car and shake me down and take every penny I had on me. Tell me to get out of the car. I've had that happen, and I didn't say nothing; I had no recourse.

In the old days we used to make a deal with the police. We knew we were going to make a deal, or the dicks knew we were going to, and they would have a lot of unsolved crimes. So, to make it easier for everybody we'd just what we called "clean the slate" for them. They'd say, "I got fifteen capers here we haven't been able to solve; will you clean them up for us?" That's all. We'd just sign a confession; I mean it wasn't really a confession. We didn't even know where these capers were. But they never used them against us or anything. It was just to clean the slate for the police department. Our attorney had probably come down and talked to us and asked us if we would do it because he wanted a favor from a policeman, or something like that. You scratch my back, I'll scratch yours. So we would go ahead and do it, knowing that they wouldn't do nothin'.

There was more principles between the thieves and the police department in those days. Now they tell me that a policeman will say yes and turn right around and do no.

When I was rooting we were very close to some policemen. In Portland we used to have to pay off twenty percent to the chief of dicks and a lot of times the guy we beat would holler for five times as much as we got and we would have to give the chief twenty percent although he knew it was wrong. You see, the criminals haven't got all the rackets; the worst ones are the upright members of society.

Every town has a criminal attorney who is the fix. The jailer would tell you who the fix in town was or the bull that pinched you because he'd get a commission from the attorney, you know, for it. Everybody wants to tell you, especially with a box man; he's usually got money so they all wanna get cut in on the action. Then they get ten percent of what the attorney gets as his fee, so you have no trouble findin' out.

The attorney will come to see you and talk to you. He asks you where you're from and usually tries to check and see if you're gonna run or not. After he talks to you a little bit, why you usually know somebody that he knows, another box man around the country or something, and he'll get you out on bail, get the bail cut down and get you out on it, or take you right out that night on bail. Then you go down and see him the next day and ask him what the score is and he'll tell you it'll cost you so much to get this cut down to a petty larceny beef and that's all there is to it. It's just that simple if the town's not hot.

If the town's hot and somebody's gotta go to the joint, if you're an outsider you're probably the one to go. But if he can beat it he flat tells you how much it'll be. He has to give the district attorney so much, and possibly the judge. It's not necessarily the district attorney; it might be an assistant in the office that he deals with. Sometimes you can square the beef in the city court and get it dropped. And the dick, if he's got a hand out why they get a piece of the action too. Everybody's got their hand out, haven't they?

You won't take off when you're out on bond because that bondsman, you see, it's like the last time; my bond was $100,000 and you didn't customarily put a thief on a $100,000 bond, but my word's good so the bondsman signed for it. You can't just take off when a guy's a right guy; you just can't take and dump him by runnin' off; that would be foolish to do, because the next time you needed a bond, you wouldn't get the bond, because they're just like safe men; I mean word gets around. Well, now I can go to New York City and tell them to call Portland and the bondsman there will tell you I'm all right. So even in New York they'll sign a bond and they'll let me out on the cuff because they know I'll go right out and go to work and get it.

Sometimes you're forced into a trial, but not usually. Only about one quarter the time. You wouldn't plead not guilty because if you're a box man and you're caught, you're right on the caper. They don't pick you up after. The [criminal] lawyer usually couldn't plead before a jury. I got a lawyer in Portland: I listened to him plead a case in the jury room one day and he almost hung this guy. And I told him afterwards, "If I ever have to go to a jury, don't you ever plead for me."

But if he's a fix, that's his field, you see; all he understands is connections. I've never found a fix that's a good trial lawyer. A fix has got it all fixed before you go to court and then the district attorney will get up and recommend this way or that way if it goes that far and you'll be granted probation, parole, or whatever they're gonna grant, or he'll ask for dismissal if you got enough money, which is a little raw so they don't very often do that. But it's all cut and dried. You know what you're gonna get before you go down to court. I've been to court hundreds of times but I've only been to prison five times.

They can't dismiss the case as a rule. It's pretty raw to do that. They suspend the sentence. They just forget about it. If you're on parole you don't necessarily stay there; it's not a good idea to stay where you were sentenced. The safe squad is usually pretty unhappy about you getting a parole and all they want to do is lock you up. Like Edgar Hoover, he says, "Commit the crime, lock him up, that's the easiest way to take care of him." And they'll roust you and give you a bad time if you've got a suspended sentence or parole, so you usually try and transfer someplace else. Of course, they don't want you there either, as soon as they find out who you are.

Sometimes you can't get the fix. You run into places, if it is real hot. I've gone into towns and looked the town over and you don't know anybody, you don't contact anybody, and some towns never publish the crime news, outside of murder or something like that, but stickups, box jobs, they don't publish them. So you go in and you don't know whether this town is red hot and you go out and root and you get snatched. You get down there; they're looking for somebody like you and nothing in the world will save you, I don't care what kind of a connection you got. People want a clean town, so they grab the first guy that they can hang on, make a big issue out of it and send him to the joint. Everybody settles down and "see what a pure town we got." The thieves that was really making the money just go on about their business.

The last time I was rootin' I used a policeman for a point man and we built such a fire in Portland, on ourselves, that when they did catch us they threw everything but the book at us. You know, and the fix was absolutely useless. I hired a fix but only to cut it down. To throw some of those beefs off me. I will show ya. My bondsman down there put up a $25,000 bond for me. I was being held in the county jail. They'd caught us cold-turkey, right out on this job by accident. A paper boy got a squint at us and my partner just as we walked across in the doorway and he called the bulls and they came out and we were completely surrounded, you know, when we came out of the joint. Half of the money disappeared in transit, but they just left us alone, you know, and let us go ahead and finish it and then come out.

Well, my lawyer came down to see me right away and he said, "I'll have Joe bail you out." Well, then, Joe was on his way up to the jail to do it when this dick that I knew came up to see me. And he told me, "They got fifty beefs down there they're going to put on you." And I said. "Man, they can't prove them beefs, none of 'em; some of them are mine and some ain't, but they can't prove them." And he said, "No, but Oregon as you know, indicts guys and lets the judge decide whether they're guilty or not." So he said, "All they've got to do is throw them down in front of the grand jury and the grand jury'll indict you." I said, "Oh, I don't think they'll do that." And Joe comes up and put his $25,000 down and before I could get out and be released, they had me on another beef at $100,000. So I bowed my neck and sent for Joe and told him, "Well, I want out." My word was good enough for him for that and he said, "All right, I'll go get the bonds and get you out." And he went down to get 'em and while he was gone, they come up and stood right there with papers for another indictment, waiting for me to get out.

So sometimes, you got to be thrown to the lions. The district attorney will resort to that; the district attorney has to have so many convictions a year. If you created a big furor in the town. My picture was in the papers for three weeks after we got pinched. And we were Number One news. That's when they can't fix it. All you can do then is try to get all the beefs throwed off except one and go to the pen for that one. That's how come you do actually go in spite of the fix. They all are in business and they have to show some results.

And with the publicity I had, well, in fact when I beat five years off the sentence and got out on probation, there was an awful storm. Why I can't even go to Portland now, you know, without them causing trouble over it. If I was still stealing I'd tear that town apart because I know I can beat 'em for a long time, I know that. But if I was going to do that, I would go from here to down there and have guys case off those joints for me and go from here down to Portland and knock 'em off and come back here and laugh at 'em. And let 'em blow their cork. But, you can't fix some of those, you just can't. And I don't mean by that that you can't fix a murder beef because you can, you know, but sometimes the heat's on too much and you just got to go ahead and go, that's all.

There's a lot of guys that do time who get real good connections and a normal beef they can fix. Two or three box men that I know in Portland went down the same way but they were small-time box men. When they finally really got nailed was when they knocked off a canteen—that has all this candy business—they got quite a large sum off that. And the canteen had a lot of strength, you know; they raised so much hell about it day after day. Where the average Hoosier believes the police department. He goes down there and says, "Well, I was robbed last night." And he goes home and says they'll catch the thief next week. The bulls know who it was so they go out and shake the guy down and get some dough off him or pinch him and the lawyer gets some dough and that's all there is to it. There is no publicity. But if it's a big beef, then everybody gets interested in it because they don't like that heat on. I've seen beefs where all the thieves get mad over it because they all got to leave town over it. And they'd all be mad at the guys that done it.

I went to prison five times and each time it was the same thing approximately. You know, too much heat. See, when I work, I work real hard. I just believe in it. I mean, it's silly to make $1,000 and go out and spend it; you're broke again. That's perpetual motion. So I don't believe that way. I say, "Well, if we're going to work, we get in a mood for everything and it is let's just keep on plowing, you know, just keep going right on down the line till we got a chunk of money, then lay off."

If you get picked up in a small town, you can deal with the D.A. personally, you know; he gets so few chances to take any dough, that when a thief comes into town, you know, why, he comes out in person and talks with him. He cuts out the attorney and everything else. I've had that happen several times, when I'd get pinched, like that. But little towns are so hard to work in because you can't case the joint off, you know. The Hoosiers know one another real well. And the bull on the beat knows everybody in town—knows where he's supposed to be and what time he's supposed to be home and what he's doing in that neck of the woods and everything else. When he sees a stranger a couple times in a evening, why right away he begins to think. And some of those little town-clowns are pretty sharp; they've been there for a long time; they get pretty sharp. They wouldn't compete with one in the city, but they're very clever in their own districts.

To give you an illustration of the fix: recently Danny was released from Montana on parole. He came to Seattle. A short time later he was arrested for possession of narcotics. He had a real sharp lawyer who could do business with the D.A. He went up and got the D.A. straightened around. After getting the case squared around they went to court. The judge was told that in as much as Danny was going to be violated and taken back to the joint they thought they should save time and money and drop the charge. The judge did this. Then the attorney for Danny flew over to Montana. He told the parole board that Danny was being held and tried for possession of narcotics in Seattle and that he thought they should continue Danny's parole. The parole board went along with the idea, not knowing that Danny had the charges dropped here. So consequently Danny remains on parole to this day, no charges against him or anything.

The fix does business with the district attorney and very seldom does he talk to the judge directly. Then when they go to court the judge usually goes along with the district attorney. Quite often the money that's given to the D.A. is split with the judge.

I automatically come in contact with corruption everywhere. But there is a great many people, judges, attorneys, policemen who are honest, extremely so, and I come in contact with the other kind; it is essential that I do. Any attorney I have is automatically a fix, which ninety percent of the criminal attorneys are, nothing but fixes. They can't take a case before a jury and win. And the policemen that I know are the policemen that will take money. The judges I know, district attorneys I know are all corrupt but I don't say they are all that way. I will say a hell of a good percent of them are. But the point is you can get a fix anywhere, Salt Lake City, Los Angeles, Las Vegas, any of them. Just find a connection, that's all.

To fix the average beef costs around $4,000 to $5,000. It would be less for petty larceny; they're not much trouble unless they have been in the bulls' hair a lot. And if they have, they want to put him away. They won't listen, you know—nobody can fix it.

In a lot of places if two men are arrested they will come up and tell you that one is going to the joint and one is going to spring. And one of the guys is going and they have to decide who it will be. Is that justice?

No, that's what is got me so mixed up—that that blindfold should be really permanently tied on there.

There is no such thing as justice in criminal courts. If you've got the money you get the fix. If you haven't got the money, you don't get it. It's just that plain and that simple. A woman set fire to her home in Portland and her father's extremely wealthy. Murder is not a bailable offense. While this woman was in jail they passed a law allowing murder to be bailed out. She was immediately bailed out and was turned loose by the jury. She deliberately set fire to her home and burned up two or three of her children. She admitted it. It was a premeditated crime, incidentally. But she was turned loose. How can you expect these guys and kids to believe that there is justice? You can't convince these kids of that when they go up there in these detention homes five or six times. Those things have to be changed.

I'll tell you a little story that I have just seen. I'm down talking to a parole officer one day pertaining to a stabbing. He said he had to take care of it right away. He was supposed to make a presentence of this guy. He sits there and reads what little information has been given to him. He determines what recommendation he is going to make to the judge. He was supposed to have personally investigated this man. I don't condemn him because he is so crowded. But the point is that he sat right there and recommended that the man be placed on probation from what he had. That's not right. That's not the answer to it.

When I was younger and the bulls would take you in you knew right then that you were gonna get a dumping [beating]. But that didn't do no good either. But right here in this police department they still give you a thumping. I know a friend of mine was killed for shooting at a policeman. They beat him so badly that when they sent him to Walla Walla he died. It was from that beating.

But as a whole there is police violence in Seattle only in a minor way, Portland in a minor way, San Francisco in a major way, L.A. in a major way only they take you to the outlying jails to accomplish it now where there is no danger of the newspapers getting ahold of it. But they will use the brutal methods. I've been through both sides of it, where they treat you with kid gloves and where they are brutal.

When I was a kid in the penitentiary they were very brutal. They threw you in a black hole and they left you there. If you made any noise three or four of them would come in and beat you up. It was very simple. There was just as much crime then as there is today.

The FBI doesn't break heads anymore at all. It's an illusion that they didn't at one time. They were just as vicious as anybody was. We go through an era, you know. Edgar Hoover is a very dedicated man. He has only one thing in this world that he wants to accomplish and that's to solve the crime and put the person in jail. That's all. He doesn't believe in parole or anything. At one time, when he first started out, he got ahold of the whip and as the boss he was a pretty vicious man. You probably don't recall, but they shot their own man one time, they were so anxious. Edgar Hoover shot at his own man one time trying to make a name for himself. They have got out of that. They have got to the point where they have become so successful that they don't need to use those methods anymore.

The only way you can beat the law is by moving all the time. The law is easy to beat as long as you keep moving. But you have to continuously move. We've proved that stealing can be very profitable by moving around all the time. I'm a great one for testing out systems and we went from right here in Seattle to Miami one time and stole ourselves silly. We made a terrific amount of money but we never was pinched once because we kept right on moving. And the FBI will tell you that as long as you keep moving, it's awfully hard for them to get you. You'll notice that they never catch any of these most wanted men till they sit down someplace. As long as those guys keep moving, they can't catch them. There's nothing for you to take ahold of, you know, to get the guy. See, you got to commit crimes and keep moving and they won't get you, unless it's just an accident. But the minute you sit down they'll get you because it's the bull's job to know all the thieves in that town. That's what makes them smart dicks.

They call these guys "camera-eye dicks." Well, that's guys that look at mug-shots all the time, men wanted here and there all around the country, and they look at them mug-shots and they walk out on the street and start lookin' around. That's why I never go down to skid road or nothing when I'm stealing. I never go but to the best places. 'Cause the bulls never go there. And I can go in town and stay there as long as I want—within reason—and then I'll never be bothered. Never.

I don't dress like a thief or pimp or anything. After I grew up and began to look around, found out that I could spot these thieves, you know, a block away the way they dressed and stuff in the old days, I quit dressing like them. I didn't think that it was so smart anymore. I was raised in what they called the "hoodlums" in San Francisco out of 16th and Mission. It was just a collection of kids—tough kids—out there. I was the only one that wasn't tough, I guess, in the whole district. But they all dressed the same. And they thought it was smart. That's when I learned not to. The bulls would come down and roust us and we didn't know how they could spot us. 'Cause we all wore the same caps and shirts. That's when I changed my style of dressing.

In the East, they stay right in one area most of the time. They stay right in New York City, it's so big. You know, they stay there. You give them a year's operation and every bull in New York will know about them, if it's in their field. But then they have the syndicate to fix it if they get busted. Out here they move around from Seattle to Portland, San Francisco to Los Angeles, Salt Lake to Phoenix, like that and it's hard for them bulls to keep up. Today they've got this teletype and stuff where they trade information and the minute they see any inkling of a guy leaving one town and going to another, they teletype it. They put that information together.

The FBI has the money to build it up and they have developed the best techniques that there are and they draw the greatest men in that field to solve a crime. They really don't have to worry anymore. Each one of their agents now is a general agent who can be turned loose on any type of crime. I wouldn't say the FBI are particularly better people. An illustration is that one of their agents in the East tried to sell some evidence that they had to some criminals. And one held up a bank in California, an ex-agent. So they are not better, but they are better with techniques. They are getting things more their way like in the fingerprint system. They are getting more laws passed that are to their benefit. This makes it easier for them to overcome laws.

If you were to read all the laws that have been sneaked in by Hoover and passed, you wouldn't believe it. You actually haven't any rights. You have violated the federal laws so many times it's pathetic. Everyone has. But in your case he doesn't want you. He wants me, the criminal. But it helps him to catch me. You would be surprised at the people who commit crimes today, businessmen who are really con men, and there is nothing they can do. Not a thing can they do to prosecute them. I'm very much against that type of crime.

The FBI has got beyond a brutal stage. They are cold-blooded; when they pull out that pistol they are going to kill you. They don't shoot at your legs or arms to cripple you. They shoot to kill. They carry that 357 magnum and no man carries a gun that big unless he intends to kill someone. That's a brutality in a sense, I guess. I don't really know if it is necessary to carry a gun. I would say offhand that it is like carrying a shotgun, but a shotgun is inconvenient and that's the only reason they don't carry one of them.

The FBI has sent policemen to schools. They have made the FBI school available. I think the school is in Washington, D.C. They have what they call a coordinator. The FBI has a man here who just hangs around the police station. All he does is coordinate between the FBI and the police.

The police department has all the reason in the world to be afraid of the FBI. They [the police] are shaking down guys all the time; prostitutes, criminals, bootleggers. So they are very much afraid of the FBI. The FBI is aware of that. It shows they overlook that. Because the policeman is there. He is there to stay. They don't dare start prosecuting the whole police department or they will get no cooperation. And no police department can get along without the stool pigeon. The city police has more access to stool pigeons than the FBI does. So the FBI, being smarter, cooperate with the city police.

No police department, FBI or otherwise, can get along without the stool pigeon. I would say that fifty percent of their crimes are solved by stool pigeons. Without them they can't get along. The FBI does not trust the city police in any manner, shape or form. I know two or three agents here real well. I've known them for years. One of them, in fact, was assigned to me at one time and tailed me around. I got tired of it and stepped in a doorway and he lost me for a minute. When he went by I told him that I was going to get a cup of coffee and why didn't we go together. That shook him up. He reminds me of it every once in awhile. Now we are pretty good friends. I also remind him once in awhile that there is a phrase in the Bible that says, "Thou Shalt Not Kill." Usually it perturbs him a great deal when I tell him that. He has no answer to it. I just do it for meanness for I know that he has to carry a gun. But that's defeat in my mind. I never carried a gun because I knew that someday I would have to kill somebody. That's what you carry a gun for. So I never carried one because I don't believe it's man's prerogative to take a life.

7

The Joint

"I don't know which came first, the chicken or the egg . . . whether the institutions created the bad criminals or the criminals created the bad institutions, but they were both very tough."

To me prison life is a case of being thrown out of society; you're thrown out of a free world and get locked up and that's all there is to it. You just like a bear hibernatin' as far as I'm concerned—you try to make your mind a blank and settle down; you have so much time to do and that's all.

My first bit in prison was in Monroe [the medium security prison in Washington]. While I was in Monroe I got in a fight one day. I picked up a file that had been sharpened to a point on one end. I stabbed a guy. I was thrown in the hole. In those days when you got put in the hole they took all your clothes, except your underwear, away from you. They gave you a wooden bench to sleep on. You were given bread and water and every third day you were given a meal, if you behaved. I was young and salty so when they would give me my bread I would throw it back in the guard's face. Consequently, I got pretty hungry. At one time I went thirty days without eating. They had to carry me out of the hole and take me to the hospital. So that cured them of putting me in the hole. They were badly scared; I was a little young then.

The authorities assigned me to the brick yard while I was in Monroe. I was put on a night shift firing the kiln for the bricks. Not liking it and trying to get off the job, I burned down the kiln one night. So I went back to the hole again. I raised a fuss there and pounded on the steel door all night and kept everybody awake all night. They took the wooden bench away from me and I had to sleep on the concrete floor. It was in the winter time and it got cold there.

Eventually, I was released from Monroe but not on parole. I went right back to stealing again because I didn't have any family by that time. I didn't think my people wanted me. So I didn't go near them. They had moved to another town that was quite aways from Monroe. I didn't have the money to get there anyhow. I went down into Oregon and stole, mostly cars and things like that. Then I went into California where my dad was. Well, he didn't seem to care anymore about me so he just let me go and do what I wanted to do. So one night, another kid and I decided to drive back to Washington. We stole a car. We got caught in the car up in Oregon and the sheriff came in and talked to me in the office. I didn't want this kid to go to jail too so I signed a confession that absolved him. I said that I had picked him up along the road. After I signed the confession the sheriff pulled another one out of his pocket and read it to me. It was almost identical to mine only that he had said that he stole the car and that he had picked me up along the road. Consequently, we both went to San Quentin.

When I arrived in San Quentin I met some guys that I had known previously. They told me that I would probably be assigned to the jute mill. It was a terrible place to work; the machinery was so old that it was always breaking down. Guys were losing fingers and things like that in the mill. They told me to refuse to work in there. They tried to put me in the jute mill and I refused so I was thrown in the hole, which was a cave in the side of a hill in the prison—damp, rats, no lights, no ventilation, never cleaned out.

Well, at that time they had a rule that any second timer could be sent to Folsom, no first timers. So when they called me in the line to talk to the captain, whose name was Handlebar Carpenter, because of a big moustache he had, I still refused to work in the jute mill. I got pretty salty about it. He told me there was a train going to Folsom today and if I didn't go in the mill I would have to go on the train. I thought he was bluffing, because I know how tough it was in Folsom. It was the toughest pen on the West Coast and still is. I didn't believe that would send me at my age, which was quite young, under twenty, to Folsom. But he wasn't bluffing and when the train went to Folsom that afternoon I was on it.

I arrived in Folsom and created quite a stir. They didn't know how to care for anyone as young as I. Everybody there was much older than me. At that time bank robbery was a state beef and they had an enormous amount of bank robbers in there and gunmen of all descriptions. It was real tough. They had me working directly under a guard on a gate as a runner. They didn't even have telephones in the institutions at that time. When they wanted a man for a visitor or one of the jobs or to see the captain they would send one runner out from the captain's office and he would come to that gate and he would tell that officer there. That officer would send his runner on. It was part of my job to know where all the guys were at in the institution and to go and get them. I worked there for a long time. Then I was put in what was called the lower yard.

Folsom is on two levels; the upper level is called the upper yard. It has all the cell houses, the dining rooms, the captain's office, hospital and the administration offices. The lower yard was an enormous quarry where everything was done by hand. All the rock was dug out. Incidentally, the whole institution at the time was made out of hand-hewn rock—all the cell houses, dining rooms, administration building, the guard houses and all. The prison officials had a racket where they sold crushed rock to the Southern Pacific Railroad. You can see today along the railroad crushed granite rock. Our job was to break that rock up into small enough pieces to go into the rock crusher. You had a quota to make every day and if you didn't make it you got sent to the hole.

They used to hang men up in straight jackets and give them croton oil and leave them hanging while it worked and it would burn the legs and butt real bad. They also would put cuffs on a man and then pull his hands up with a rope until his feet were just flat on the floor and leave him all day and that is very painful after a few hours.

While in the lower yard, I became acquainted with a clique of men who hung out together. All were professional bank robbers or robbers of some type. There were about six or eight of them in this clique. They ate together, stayed in the same cell house. The captain let me alone because none of this clique was homosexual. That relieved him of the pressure of watching me all the time or having me watched to keep the homosexuals from bothering me. This clique wouldn't let anybody touch me or get near to me. I knew everything that was going on, all the escape attempts and the narcotics coming into the institution. I got quite an education out of it.

We used to have a knifing there at least once a week and there was somebody killed in there at least once in three months by a knife. I've seen a great many knife fights; I've seen lots of guys get killed by knives. I never saw them use a club or anything; it was always a knife. In fact, almost everybody in the institution carried a knife for protection.

One of the comical incidences was that we had a swimming pool in the bath house in the upper yard where we took our baths. No one in the history of the institution could remember the swimming pool ever being filled with water for the inmates. In fact we used to take our clothes off down there because there wasn't room enough up on the level where the showers were. So this day somebody discovered that the swimming pool was full of water. We heard that Hiram Johnson, the state senator, was coming through the institution to visit. So the guard had to leave for some reason. The guys picked the lock on the door in the bathroom. When the guard came back the swimming pool was full of guys swimming. They had quite a time getting them out of the water.

Guys used to have grudge fights with knives in this dried swimming pool by tying their left hands together with a handkerchief. It sounds like a vicious thing but it isn't. They would cut one another. But when one man would leap toward the other, the second man would pull away. Consequently, he would pull the first guy off balance. You could never push the knife clear in; you could only make a cut on a person. Those guys would get badly cut up but they would never kill one another. It was usually done by premeditation. The guys would get in an argument in the lower yard and say, "Well on Saturday I will meet you in the bath house." Somebody would make arrangements to get the guard outside while the guys had the fight. I saw several of those while I was in. But I never saw anybody killed in that type of fight. I've seen them very badly cut all over their body. Usually when two guys got into a fight out in the yard they would take their coat or shirt off and wrap it around their left arm so they could use it defensively to protect their body from cuts of the knife. They would let the man stab into this cloth and into their arm in preference to having him stab into their body. It worked quite successfully. In the meantime it would be like two boxers.

We were dressed in blue denims. We had men there who were dressed in black and white stripes. They were considered the most dangerous men in the institution. Whenever there was any trouble in the yard the guards had strict orders to shoot the guy in the black and white stripes first. Then go ahead and shoot anybody else. That was an order discussed by guards and inmates both.

We had one real large tower that was built out of hand-hewn stone right down in front of the administration building. In the base of it were six cells. I was in the institution for three and a half years. There were guys in those cells that I had never seen; they had never been out of them in all that time. They had been in there for years for violating some rule, like an escape or a knifing or something like that.

The ordinary holes where they put the men were in the back alley. It was the back end of a cell house. The door was a solid steel door. When they closed the door it was coal black in the cell. I committed some violation of the rules one time and was put in there. I had heard about this before so I tried it: to take, when they feed you, your plate of beans, which was what you got every night; why I saved out about a half dozen beans, I believe it was ten. I let them dry out. It's extremely hot in that area. When the beans dry you take them and throw them in the air. This is a small cell, remember. There is nothing in there except a bucket for a toilet. No water, no nothing. You throw these beans in the air and let them come down. You know how many there are. The idea is to find them all. Believe me, you cannot find them all. You are in the dark there and you keep feeling around on the floor and you cover the same area continuously. You think you are in a new area and you're not. To keep from going crazy, that's what the guys do in there.

There is no sound or nothing in there. They can just vaguely hear the guys going into their cells and out of their cells and that's all they can hear. It's a solid steel door and a rock building. No light at all ever gets in. I would spend hours and hours and hours hunting for these beans and couldn't find them all. Once a week they would take and come down with a stool pigeon trustee and they would mop out your cell. And sure enough, he would sweep up two or three beans that you couldn't find. Sometimes you would even be tempted to feel on the walls to see if the bean had stuck there. But it didn't because it was dry.

The Folsom food was outrageous. We got oatmeal for breakfast without milk and one spoonful of sugar on it everyday. The only thing that was any good was the bread. It was homemade. The guys ate lots of it. You could have all you wanted. At noon you usually got codfish stew, which was made from the fat of the meat. The guards got all the meat and you got all the fat and potatoes. They had a large farm there and they raised stuff out there. Then on Sunday, you got two meals a day. You got mush for breakfast and then in the afternoon you would get roast beef. And that's all you got. Three hundred and sixty-five days out of the year. They didn't recognize Thanksgiving, Christmas or anything else.

At that time there were no radios or TVs. We had phonographs. They allowed us to have a phonograph in a cell. It would be shipped in from the outside. At night you would have a couple of hundred men in the cell house and there would be twenty of them playing a phonograph. The cells were all open faced with bars on them. If you didn't have a phonograph to drown out the other guys you would have to listen to five or six songs within you radius going at one time. If there was nothing else to drive you crazy, that would.

We didn't have a great number of homosexuals in Folsom. There were some. But most of it was by natural queers, the guys that played the part of a girl. So they didn't fit in there. There was more of it in San Quentin than there was in Folsom. There were younger people in San Quentin. These guys were all older in Folsom. They didn't go in for it. There's very few homosexuals in penitentiaries. In the lesser places it's quite common—like in reformatories. But when you get into the tougher penitentiaries they have grown to the age where they know what they want. There are some who will float or generate toward that person, will pull toward them automatically, but they're a minority. And the one who plays the part of the female is definitely in a minority. There's very few of them there. The queers on the street very seldom wind up in penitentiaries unless they are a thief.

At Folsom there was a canal that ran through from a dam up above the institution. A river runs right alongside of it. This canal was built by inmates and so was the dam. It was made of hand-hewn rock. The canal ran into a power house in the lower yard and turned this generator and then went on out. At the lower end of the canal, right where the wall came down to the canal, was a guy named Tony. He was considered pretty crazy. He was a crack shot. He used to shoot at any box or anything that was thrown into the canal. If the guys wanted to have some fun they would throw a small box in the water and when it came by Tony why he would shoot it. The reason for that was the guys used to get in the canal and take a piece of rubber hose and breath out of it and put rocks in their pockets to hold them down. They would float down underneath Tony's tower. After they got beyond there they could climb out anyplace and they would be free. Instead of putting a metal net across there why they just put Tony in the tower. He took care of it. He had killed two or three guys who attempted to escape in that manner.

At that time if you would get a pistol and turn it in, you would be paroled. It had been done several times by guys who had people from the outside smuggle pistols in to them. They would turn it in as having found it.

In 1927 on Thanksgiving day, there were five or six guys: Eddie Stuart, Tony Brown, and I don't recall the rest of the names, had gotten ahold of this pistol. They had decided to kidnap this warden and go out of the front gate. Well they missed. This all went on during a picture show. The picture show was in a building completely surrounded by windows. It was used as a library during the week. It had about two hundred volumes in it of books that had been given to them. Nobody ever went in there to read them or anything.

At the middle of the show Tony Brown and Eddie Stuart went out and kidnapped the guard on the gate and beat him to death. They went down the cell house end to a door that went into the administration building. They stayed out of sight until an inmate who was a trustee started to go through that door. They tried to get through there at the same time. The guard was too fast for them and slammed the door shut. So they came back and they killed two or three guards. I can't remember their names. They (the inmates) beat one guard to death so badly that you couldn't recognize his head from hamburger. Ray Singleton was his name. He was rated as one of the best guards in the institution.

In the meantime, the warden had called out the National Guard. They arrived from Sacramento and completely surrounded this library and theater and set up machine guns. All the inmates of the institution were in this building. They sent down a warning that if these guys didn't give up they were going to shoot into the building. These guys thought they were bluffing and they were trying to think up some way to get out. So they refused. And sure enough they shot in there. I saw guys shot right and left—there was shooting through all the windows. I was lying on the floor and I could see, just as if a sewing machine were running across a motion picture machine, little holes appearing. Looked just like somebody was sewing with a sewing machine. Somehow or other, I wasn't injured in it.

We stayed in there all that night and the next morning these guys gave up. They were taken down and tried in Sacramento for murder. They were sentenced to be executed. At that time, the scaffold for hanging people was erected right in the cell house where the inmates to be executed were kept. Normally, they would take the inmate out the back alley and put him in one of those cells down there. They would have a screen door on it and have a guard sit right in front of the door watching him while they erected the scaffold over the hanging room. But when Tony and those guys were in there, the guards hated them so bad that they erected the scaffold right when they were in the cells facing it. There was no way they could miss it. There were no windows they could look out. Just this open door and when they looked out of it they saw where they were erecting the scaffold.

When they erect the scaffold they test it with ropes and heavy weights. The guards were there testing it all the time. Tony Brown and those guys were sitting in their cells watching it. But they were pretty tough kids and it didn't seem to affect them any. They executed all of them except one who had turned state's evidence.

We had a great many food riots there. All the guys would take their food and throw it all over the dining room. All the guards did, who were on the floor, was walk out, lock the door. The guards up on the cat walk around the top of the building would shoot down in there and wound two or three guys. It would then be over. I could never understand that. It was the most foolish thing in the world. We never won any of them. We always lost; somebody always got shot.

No women were ever allowed inside in any part of the institution at anytime. It was out of bounds for women, that's how tough that joint was.

We had two or three guys in there who had been stagecoach robbers. That's how far back it was [1927]. These guys had been in there for years. They were pretty old at that time. But they were still tough old men.

I watched one of the guys in our clique that had gotten in a beef with another guy. This fellow in our clique was extremely dangerous. He had no fear of anything. He believed that a gun or a knife was a way to settle a beef. This happened on a Saturday. I knew that he was going to get this guy so I followed him around all afternoon to see what was going to happen. He finally got this guy on a bench. He just slipped up, sat down beside the guy, ran the knife into him and got up and walked away. He was at least fifteen or twenty feet before the guy set up a cry. They never did catch the guy who did the knifing.

I believe that the criminals at that time were much tougher than they are today. They were very vindictive and had nothing to lose. So many of them were doing natural life. I found that in all institutions with the exception of Monroe where they were too young. They were just tough kids. But once you got in San Quentin or Folsom they were bad, real bad. They were treated badly.

I don't know which came first, the chicken or the egg. It was the same with those criminals. I don't know whether the institution created the bad criminals or the criminals created the bad institution, but they were both very tough. The guards were tough and brutal. They used to beat up on the guys all the time. The cons would kill the guards when they got the opportunity or would let something fall on them or something like that. We had two or three guards in the institution who were well liked by the majority of the inmates. They were good people. But as a whole, I guess the word is sadistic. The guards were terrible.

I remember one incident that happened. Two guys got into a beef. One of them was in the barber shop getting his hair cut. The other guy sneaked into the barber shop behind him and took a knife and just about cut his head off. That took care of the beef.

A railroad ran into the lower yard in order to haul out this crushed rock. The oil cars that furnished oil for the institution were brought in on the same railroad. Then it was transferred to a smaller tanker and pulled by cable up an incline into the upper yard. One Sunday morning I was at the winch and was having coffee when three young kids about twenty-five came in there. They had just been given life sentences for armed robbery. They just made up their minds that they couldn't do it. Facing this incline was about five guard towers with machine guns. It was strictly taboo to be on this incline at anytime. There was no fence or nothing. You just better not get caught on it. These three kids started running down there and I was standing there watching. You could see them jerking end over end from these machine guns shooting at them. I guess that they were so full of lead that they could hardly pick them up.

I found out from a friend of theirs that they had just made up their minds they couldn't do their time. They decided to commit suicide and that was the most practical way because the most towers would be aimed toward them. Normally, during the week, these towers would be watching the whole lower yard but there was nothing to watch except the incline on Sunday.

Everyone in the institution smoked Bull Duram. There was nothing tailor-made in there. We had a commissary day in there once a month and that's all. You were allowed $5 a month. We got everything wholesale. It bought quite a little bit. Enough to last you a whole month. Guys bought candy bars and things like that. They shaved with ordinary soap and all they bought was a blade for their razors.

When we lined up to go in at night, well we had a great many Mexicans in the institution. I've seen guys standing in line with a sack between their legs resting on the ground, a Mexican in back of them cutting the whole back out of their sack and stealing all the commissaries. Like I say, I've never seen a place like that before or since. They had more guts for things like that than anything I've ever seen.

The hangman of the institution was named Bredigee. They had to keep him in the tower he was so vicious. He loved to hang the guys. He would shoot anybody whenever they went near that tower. You had to walk extremely carefully and not run or he would shoot right now.

No matter what a guy died from, nobody investigated. If his body was shipped home, which was very unusual, it was always in a sealed coffin. They would hold the body there until it was necessary to seal the coffin right at the institution. Then they would ship it home and warn the parents or relatives not to open the coffin.

You must remember that most of these guys who were in Folsom, Salem, etc., in those years were outcasts from their family. They had been gone many years from their people. So when they died there was nobody to notify. The cons didn't write to anybody while they were alive. So whatever they died from the doctor would just say it was an accident, a heart attack, or something like that, or that he had been beaten to death by inmates.

Each institution was a city in itself. The governor or mayor was the warden. Whatever he did was alright with the doctor or any of the guards in the institution. He was the Lord Mayor.

Make no mistake. I tell you that I don't think that there's much brutality in police departments today but there still is in penitentiaries. They still have just as much brutality as they did last year or the year before. I talked to guys all the time just got out of Walla Walla and they tell me that for the hardcore inmate, they throw him in the hole and beat him up just the same as they always did. Or they put them in solitary confinement; that's an easy way for the warden to handle them.

I was released from Folsom after five years; although my sentence was five years, you usually only do three years and four months. But they kept me anyhow. I don't remember why. I was placed on parole, although I had done my complete sentence. They gave me $10 on my release and a ticket to San Francisco from Folsom. I went down to San Francisco and reported to the parole officer. It was the only time I saw him until I finally went to him and asked him about a discharge, which he gave me. The parole system was very lax in those days; all they wanted you to do was stay away from them. If you left them alone, they would leave you alone. Very few guys were violated unless they committed a crime and were placed in jail. Then the parole officer would have to act. But if you stayed away from the police and kept your nose clean, they would never bother you at all.

As I said, I only received $10 when I got out. It didn't last very long. Even in those days it wouldn't pay for meals and room for any length of time at all. So I had no alternative except to turn to crime. I had a good send in with people in San Francisco who were in the upper echelon of crime. I immediately went to them and talked to them. They steered me around and got me fixed up with an apartment and things like that. They gave me money to get by on.

I went to work for a guy named Black Tony. He was the biggest narcotic peddler on the Pacific Coast. Because of my age, no one would suspect me of being a runner for narcotics. It used to be my job to go and make the pickup because he trusted me and because of the recommendations that I had from these other people. I would go and pick up suitcases full of morphine. In those days heroin was unknown. As you know it comes from opium and it's turned into morphine and from morphine into heroin. At that time, as near as I can remember, there was no such thing as heroin on the market.

I worked for him for quite awhile and he was a good guy to work for. He gave me a liberal amount of money and most anything I wanted. In the meantime, I would go out with these young guys and we would steal. That was the first time that I was shot. One night we stole a radio and some other things. The next morning we decided to take the radio to the pawn shop and peddle it. I had a car that was given to me by Black Tony. So we parked the car downtown and got out. One of the guys was carrying the radio. We went down this alley and at the mouth of the alley I stopped and looked up and down the street. Just then there was a volley of shots fired up the street. One of them ricocheted off the side of the alley and hit me in the arm. I thought that the policemen were shooting at me because we had this stolen radio. Actually he was shooting at some guys that had stuck up the bus depot.

Thinking that the police were firing at me, I couldn't go to a hospital or anything. I dropped the radio and ran back to the car. I went to my apartment. I was living with a girl at the time. She dressed it and tried to fix it up but it was pretty bad. The slug had flattened out when it had hit the other side of the building. Somebody went and got this quack doctor. So he dressed it, fixed it up, and the next day gangrene set in. He came and looked at it and said he couldn't treat me any further, the arm had to be amputated. I was deathly afraid that I would be sent back to Folsom. I told this girl to go into the dresser and get a 38 pistol that was there to sit right there and not let anybody take me out of there. I knew I was going to go off my head. She sat there for seven days, never left the apartment, and took care of me. At the end of seven days I came out of it. The doctor hadn't been back or anything. Just one of those things. Her cleaning the wound and taking care of it the way the doctor told her to got me well. I still have this scar on my right forearm.

All in all, I was shot five times in my life. One night these other guys and I decided to root the landlady of a whorehouse out in the Filmore district. We went out there; her apartment was on the top floor. Nobody went up there except when she went up there at night. She had a large quantity of furs and jewelry. We knew where they were; they were locked in a wardrobe steamer trunk. We sneaked upstairs, got by the maid. We broke into this apartment and threw the trunk out of the window. It landed down on the cement floor below. The other two kids had already gone down there and I threw it out. They gathered up all the stuff and we took it down to this fence, who was a well-known businessman in San Francisco, highly respected. He owned a large jewelry store there. There was an enormous amount of jewelry and furs in this stuff. He said, "I'll give you $19,000 apiece." He said he only had $19,000 so I took that. I was kinda the leader I guess. So I took my $19,000. Later, the jeweler reevaluated this merchandise and only gave my partners $17,000 apiece. He tried to get back a couple thousand from me, but he couldn't.

A few years later I was arrested in Oregon and sent to Salem. When I went to Salem I was placed in the hospital. Having no money in the institution, I looked around for some means for buying cigarettes. We had a water still in the laboratory there and I discovered that some of the medicines we got had a high percentage of alcohol in them. It all came in gallon jugs. We had an old doctor there who was retired from practice in Portland. I would get one of the other guys to turn him around, and while he had his back to me I would steal a couple of jugs of this medicine. I put it in the lab and after they locked up the main line I would start my still up and run the alcohol out of it. I would sell it in the yard the next day for cigarettes. I did quite well until I finally sold to a stool pigeon. He turned me in with a pint of alcohol. So I was taken out of the hospital. For some unknown reason, they didn't put me in the hole. They just took me off the job.

While I was in the hospital, there was a riot in the yard one day. They brought a couple of guys up who were shot. One kid was shot in the hand and the other guy was shot in the chest. They put him on the operating table and the doctor took care of the guy with the injured hand, which figures; at his age he would do that. He told me to give the guy on the table artificial respiration. I did. I was growing tired of it. I called the doctor in and told him that the guy looked awfully bad. He looked at the guy and checked his heart and said I was trying to pump air into a dead man. This guy had been dead for some time, I guess.

I have always been a fairly good prisoner. I am capable of realizing that you can't win in these institutions by fighting them. I often marvel at some of the criminals who seem so intelligent and have such high I.Q.s and who fight them all the time. They continuously fight them from the day they enter the institution until they leave.

You get up and go to breakfast, which is normal, and then you usually go to the yard for recreation. They all go out there and that gives them an opportunity to visit the doctor's line or anything like that. They do no good but everybody gets into the doctor's line anyhow. The doctor just gets madder and madder and keeps lookin' down the line all the time. Then you go back, after you got in the doctor's line, you go back in the yard. The guys are usually gambling out in the yard. They gamble all the time; I mean it's an outlet, that's really all it is. And then you go on to the shop and you go to work, whatever shop you're assigned to.

In Salem this last time I was assigned to the furniture shop. I hate to say it because I hate him so bad, but this warden that they have in Salem is in my estimation one of the best wardens I've ever seen. He was trained in the federals by the federals. He was assistant warden in the federal institution. He's an ornery old bastard, too, to get along with. But he was a very honest man and there's a lot of connivin' goes on in a prison. I think that you can understand that. You lock up five hundred thieves, they're gonna be connivin' around. They steal anything they can lay their hands on, especially if it's food. They cook up a bunch of chicken or something, you know, steaks; when they go to serve 'em they've disappeared just as fast as they can cook 'em.

In Salem, one time a guy made a score. They had a canteen, a commissary; you can go down there every week and if you've got money on the books you can buy, which everybody gets paid in the institution a small amount. I think it's 50 cents a day, but it's enough to keep you in smokes. One day a canteen manager, who was a free man and a bull, went down there and tried to get in the canteen and he couldn't. Right away he became suspicious and waited till the regular bull in that area went by and he stopped him and told him. He said, "Call up the Captain and tell him to send somebody down there; there's something the matter with the lock here." There was somethin' the matter with it; they had it jammed and there was a guy inside prowling. The guy had picked the lock and he was prowlin' the canteen.

Like I say, the warden's very strict but very fair; conniving is to the minimum. If you got a steak coming, you're going to get that steak. See, them joints where they just let them get away with it, stealing that stuff, wind up that half the main line gets steak and the rest of 'em don't get nothin'. This warden takes care of that; he sees to it that they cut it down to a minimum. Every guy is issued the same clothing; there's no "bonnarue" [from "bonnet rouge," which French trustees once wore], a guy all fixed up, fancy, one guy. His houseboy—it's just a very good illustration—his houseboy, he eats on the main line with the rest of the guys. Never been heard of in the penitentiary before. They always eat right there at the warden's house. Not him; his houseboys go in and eat with the rest of us in the main line. They wear main line clothes just the same as every man in the joint wears the same identical clothing, just like if you were in the service.

I have a terrific animosity toward the type of people they hire in these penitentiaries. They pay them the lowest salary there is and get the lowest type labor. And they get very personal picking on guys and things like that to debase a man.

They gamble a great deal in the penitentiary to pass the time and they use cigarettes as a means of exchange, exclusively. I understand that they have changed to Pall Malls—it used to be Camels. But I was talking to a guy a while back; he told me that they smoke Pall Malls, and I never use Pall Malls. Why I don't know.

You'd be surprised how men in the penitentiary gain knowledge pertaining to how [athletic] teams are doing or what their potential is for the next year and they bet on it. Some of those guys positively become wizards. They make a living out of it outside, just gambling on that. Course on the other hand, they had that regular hours, regular food and everything in there that lets them study with a clear mind where if they were outside, they would have other things to contend with; then they probably couldn't think as clearly in picking their teams. But some of those guys do real well at it and they follow baseball, football, fights and basketball too, quite a bit.

Not long ago we went down to Corvallis where they were having a play-off. Seattle was playing and I seen about eight or ten guys I knew in the joint down there at the game.

When I went to Salem this last time the warden there believed that everybody in the institution should work to keep them out of trouble. He had made arrangements, irregardless of the unions, to make all the furniture—chairs, desks, couches, tables, beds—for other state institutions. This saved the state a great deal of money. I was placed in the cabinet shop, mill it was called. I learned how to make chairs. When I first went in there I thought it was outrageous. But after I was there a little bit I found out there was so much about a chair that I never knew before. Before I just thought you pulled up a chair and sat down. I learned that there were heights from the floor, definite size seats to a chair that accommodate all people. I got interested in it and read some books on it that the mill superintendent loaned me.

I worked in the mill pretty near all the time I was there. I'm not sure, but I think that had a bearing on my going straight when I was released. I think for the first time in my life that I was going out of an institution with a trade, something I could fall back on. I found out that there were several places in Portland that made furniture and I could probably get a job there. Like I said, I think, though I'm not sure, that that had a bearing on my going straight.

The only drawback in all of this was that in the institution we made everything by hand. Labor was cheap; we got 50 cents a day. They were in no hurry to get it made. They always had a lot of time; there were no deadlines or contracts. When I got out I went to a furniture dealer in Portland by the name of Cohen and asked him for a job in his plant. He said sure and told me to go out there and see the superintendent. I went out there and looked at some of the modern machinery that they were using. Of course, they were paying the union scale for these men so they had to produce a great amount of furniture everyday. I went into the chair department where I thought I was familiar. I found out where we turned out ten chairs a day in the institution they were turning out a thousand chairs a day. So I became very disillusioned.

By the way, I have found that the Jewish race is the one race that will give an ex-con a job it it's available before any other race will.

Why, I don't know, whether they have been persecuted for centuries or what. I don't know why. I have found that they don't care if you are an ex-con or not. They will put you to work.

In prison everyone dreams about women. They dream so much about marriage and a home and all that, and when they come out they think all they have to do is go on into it; the majority are not capable of sitting down and analyzing. They jump into something without any thought at all. And the results are—an unhappy marriage. They just got to be unhappy; it makes sense to anyone who thinks about it.

Now I think that a guy in prison should be the same as anybody else. Should be made to earn his way through. The average con spends sixteen months in a state penitentiary. How in the hell can they be sending guys to the joint for twenty years and stuff like that? I'll tell you why. I don't even have to go over there. I don't even have to ask how many guys are at the joint; it's overcrowded. When it gets overcrowded, they turn them loose. That's a hell of a system, ain't it? These guys should be made to go into penitentiaries and be given the proper tests, whatever they might be, and then be on their own to prove they're ready for the outside world.

And the way the system works now, every joint is identical. I don't care where you go, Timbuctoo or what. They ring the bell in the morning and you get up; they ring another bell, you go eat—you can do it every morning at the same time. You don't have to do nothing; all you have to do is put your clothes on. You have no initiative, your time is going to go on. You're going to get out just the same as the guy that works like heck. Fact, lots of times they turn toublemakers out just because they want to get rid of them. These guys should be taken over there and given proper examinations and things like that to place them in the right place instead of putting all this money in these parole officers here and having a big suite of offices in some fancy building, which I imagine is a little expensive and political appointees to put these guys on the parole board that don't know nothin' about it. In the first place, they should never have a policeman on a parole board. That's the last thing they should have.

When I went to the penitentiary, I'll tell ya, the last time I did time, they put me in the furniture factory. It might sound silly but as I said, I was happier 'n hell in there. I done that time the easiest I ever did it. I wound up foreman in the furniture factory, 'cause I liked it. The only unfortunate part about it was I went to Portland and tried to go to work in them furniture factories and I couldn't. I didn't know what they was doing. I could handmake that, see, but I couldn't compete with those machines. That's what you have to do, give these guys a chance to compete. Let them get out here and make their living for theirself and I think you will save a percentage—a darn good percentage—of them. You won't be saving them, you'll be letting them save theirself. Let the guy earn his way out there by doing it properly, you know.

My parole officer's got so much work to do that, nothing personal but I lived in one place for three years, I still live there, and for two years and a half I never saw my parole officer and he's supposed to come at least once a month and visit my place of residence but the man just couldn't do it. As long as he has to operate in this manner, as long as I cause no trouble, don't get arrested or anything, they leave me alone and go to the kids, you know, that are causing him trouble. That's not the right way to do it. A system has got to be run.

Like I was told here in a very good illustration: the teacher said, "Now if you go over to the University you got to go right by the book." That's the way it all should be. Every bit of it. This guy should come and see me. I don't feel hurt about it. It makes no difference. I'm going to do the parole if I want to, if I don't want to I ain't going to. 'Cause if I can't outsmart a parole officer, well I better give up. 'Cause he's not trained in detecting crimes.

But I think that they should change their system so he's not a parole officer anymore. He's spent all his time in jail interviewing guys and stuff like that. That's not right. They should be helping the guy that wants to be helped. They'll indicate it, that's the important point. Any man will indicate if he finds something that's of interest. I went into this furniture factory and I couldn't even chop kindling wood when I went in there. Gees, I'm looking at this stuff. They let you wander around three or four days you know, cause cons are pretty aversive to work. I went around and I got interested in chairs, and I liked it. I'd go back in the cell that night and say, "What's the matter with you, what you monkeying with those chairs for? You're a thief." See, but I liked it.

If somebody had taken me twenty years ago and done that why I think I'd done all right then. I cost society a lot of money. The taxpayers. What I'd say to do is to take them off the rock pile, buy these guys modern machinery to teach 'em over there—teach them so they can compete outside. It's just as imperative that you teach the white guys who are having trouble as it you teach the Negroes and bring them up.

I'm not against that, don't misunderstand me, I'm either way, I just wait and see which way the ball's going to bounce, here. But if they're going to go it with something like that why don't they take—you've got as many white guys in jail as you've got Negro population I'd say offhand. So why not do something for them instead of saying, "He done time. He's a criminal. He's an excriminal." That don't help.

Did you ever stop to think they try to help drunks, they try to help hypes—but no one tries to help excons—I mean really try in a follow up not just while they are in the joint but when they get out to fit in with the training period of the incarceration—and the cons and excons cost the taxpayer the most money.

This guy I know served twenty two years in the joint. He went from Missouri out here. The church helped him moving around, trying to make up his mind where he wanted to go. He had got married right after he had got out, which in my conception is seeking something that you dreamt about for a long time, you know, and it works a little different than that. You don't just come out and marry some woman, sayin' what the hell—that ain't going to work. You know, you have to get straightened out yourself and he married this girl in Chicago, I believe it was, and then they gave him money to come here. He stayed here a month. He was worried that someone would discover that he had done time. He was bugged on it, you know. And when I talked to him for the Padre,* I told him, "Man, you ain't going to meet them people, you'll get a jacket pretty quick and it's going to come out so you might as well tell them now and get it over with." And I said, "Your type of guy is going to worry; I do the same thing; every time folks show up around wherever you're working, you're going to think this is it. And me, I tell 'em when I walk down the street, when I see the bull, they give the finger on me, that's all; I got nothing to hide." They finally got money from the Father and went back East again. Totally lost out here. We each could be lost back there, too.

---

*A local priest who was Harry's friend.

8

Rehabilitation

"We each could be lost back there, too."

When a guy comes out of an institution, especially an old-timer, adjustment to society and what you call a normal life is extremely hard for him. I don't feel that the process sets in for about three months after he gets out; then he begins to look around. Up till that time, until three months is up, why he's so busy duckin' traffic and tryin' to get adjusted to his job and things like that that he really doesn't look around. But after ninety days, why he begins to look around and sees the traffic whizzin' by and identifies the cars as individual cars, not just a group of monsters that he has to be wary of all the time.

First you must remember that, as a professional criminal, I was not a member of society, was not accepted by society, was rejected by them. So now I have to turn around and change my way of thinking and think the way the people of society do. An illustration was: I worked in a small hospital in Portland as a maintenance man and I see things goin' on in the hospital all the time by the doctors, where they take people who've got some minor ailment, check them in the hospital, put 'em to bed, sometimes even operate on them when an operation wasn't called for at all and the people could ill afford it—they weren't covered by any insurance or anything and had to pay for it out of their pocket. I saw nurses take and give patients a shot of distilled water and tell the patients that it was a hypodermic and they would take the hypodermic pill, a narcotic, with them; saw nurses who were addicted to narcotics in a mild way. All these things I had to place on the side of society.

I'm a member of society now but all those things took place on my side of the fence where we cheated everybody 'n took everything we could get ahold of, stole it. And now on this side of the fence, why we're supposed to be holy. So we're told, and we find that we're not, that people are more thieves on this side of the fence than there is on the other side.

The criminal element is the minority and society is the majority so I found that there were more thieves and cheaters, racketeers on the society's side of the fence than there was a criminal, actual criminal, lawbreaker, on the other side, and frankly I have never really got adjusted to it. I don't quite understand it. I'm sure that someone has an explanation, but I have none.

One thing that I have always believed, that when a man was arrested, convicted, sentenced to a penitentiary or an institution of some kind, that he paid his debt to society and then when he came out of the institution that his record should be clean, not erased, but just clean. But when I came out the police hounded me continuously, trying to run me out of Portland or find some cause to rearrest me and send me back to the institution. One detective that hated me extremely bad made the comment that if he ever caught me in a dark alley, he was going to leave me there, meaning that he was going to kill me.

If I'm stealing I expect these things, but when I'm not stealing and am attempting to go straight why I expect them to halfway understand anyhow and leave me alone, not hound me as they did. They put a prowl car in front of my apartment at night an' things like that, have 'em sit there all the time. The neighbors discussed it, didn't understand why the prowl car was sitting there with two harness-bulls* in it. I knew why, and I used to laugh at 'em because I'd go out the back way of this apartment house and over the fence and then go on up the street about my business and come back in the same way and they wouldn't even know I'd left the house.

The police went to the doctor in the hospital and told him that I was stealin', which I wasn't, and the doctor knew I wasn't, knew I was tryin' to go straight. So he didn't believe 'em but he could have very easily and fired me.

I found in this normal world that there was a great deal of throat-cutting going on all the time. Everybody seemed to have an axe to grind and if you didn't cater to the right people, why you were in trouble. Being of an independent nature, why I figured that all I had to do was do my work and that was all and people would realize that and

---

*Policemen with guns under their coats.

leave me alone. But that wasn't the case. They wanted me to kowtow to 'em and they all knew that I'd done time, and I quite often laughed at some of the nurses and doctors who looked down on me. Some of the doctors came to me and propositioned me, that if I knew somebody that was real solid people and they wanted a prescription filled for narcotics why the doctor would do it, at a very high price of course. And still this doctor would look down on me. He didn't speak to me normally unless he had to; treated me like I was, I don't know, a slave or servant or something on that order.

Don't misunderstand me; there were a lot of understanding people too that didn't know much about ex-cons and were a little bit fearful but still they were good people. They tried to understand and tried to help; I found a lot of them like that. It made no difference to them. Like the Negro problem, they tried to understand that and the skin, the color of the skin made no difference to them. In the same way with my past, they considered that it was gone, that I was trying to get established as a square-john so they tried to help me.

I quit the hospital and went to work on another job and the police immediately went out and saw the boss and talked to him and told him that I was a criminal and that I had only one reason for being there. In fact there was nothing to steal there that was worth stealing but they told this man that that's what I'd eventually do and that I was a dangerous criminal and things like that, and they got him so upset that he came to me and talked to me about it and he didn't want to can me and he didn't want to keep me. So I just told him that the best thing to do was for me to quit because he was a nice guy and that I didn't want to cause him no trouble, which relieved his mind considerably when I told him that, so I left.

This went on for several jobs. Now these were all small companies. An extremely large company—United States Steel, Bethlehem Steel, Todd Shipyards, Lockheed, Boeing's—why the police can't bulldoze those kind of people; those people are too intelligent for them and the police have to leave you alone when you work for them. They'll harass you in other ways, like when they see you going down the streets, stopping and shaking you down or arresting you for investigation or things like that. But the big companies cannot be bothered. But, unfortunately, I was going to work for small companies and this harassment went on for three or four jobs until I was on the point of giving up.

I had a parole officer who was a personal friend of this detective who hated me so bad that when I'd get a new job, why the parole officer would tell this detective and he'd immediately go out, or send somebody out, to talk to my boss about it. And even though I had told the boss beforehand that I was an ex-con, why they would lay such a big story on him that he'd get all shook up about it.

In fact, once that I know of, they had the boss so shook up that he thought his life was in danger if he corrected me or anything in my work, and I couldn't stand that so I went to him and told him that I quit and then asked him what the score was and he told me. He'd never come in contact with an ex-con before and he was pretty nervous about it and the fact that I carried a pistol all the time, which I couldn't prove to him that I didn't because he believed the police department—which is normal; he's a member of society, he's supposed to respect the police department as honorable people. And he believed what they said against what I said so I left there too.

Because ex-cons trying to go straight are in the minority, they're an unknown quantity and everybody's afraid of the unknown, or the majority of people are. And that's why it's so hard to make owners of companies, bosses, understand that maybe these guys are trying to go straight, especially when the police department goes to them and tells 'em that the guy isn't, that he has an ulterior motive in whatever he's doing, that he has no intention of going straight.

Eventually, I couldn't stand the pressure in Portland and came to Seattle. Came up here, went through the same thing. You go out to a company, you fill out an application, and invariably the application says, "Have you ever done time?" You fill out the application and you say, "Yes." You try to minimize it if you can.

But when you hand the application to the personnel manager, why you watch him very closely and as he reads down. You see when he comes to it. He'll stop reading almost and read it over two or three times, the part about being an ex-con, and invariably he'll look up to you, at you, and then continue reading.

And you feel frustrated; you feel, "Well, here we go again." And nine times out of ten, "Here we go again."

I filled out a great many of these applications and actually had the job from talking with the boss because of my experience and whatever, or needing me, and then when I filled the application out they turned me down on some pretext; they'd call me later or something on that order. And that's real hard for a con; he loses face. All this conversation about we're going to give an ex-con a break and help him out and all that, why he begins to think that this is a bunch of hooey. I guess I never will get my debt paid to society. I'm going to have to carry this cross for the rest of my life.

One thing about going to work for the [federal] government is all they demand from you is that you put down every day that you did in an institution or every arrest you had, and that's all. They don't judge you by that. They accept you just the same on your work qualifications. And that's more than any of the rest of 'em will do. Even the big companies dislike very much to hire ex-cons. The rule is breaking down a little bit at a time, but they have a rule that says "no."

I was talking to a guy the other day that manages for a chain of shoe stores, clear across the United States, an exceptionally big chain. A guy came in who had quite a bit of experience in shoes and the manager wanted to hire him, and he was telling me about this, knowing I'm an ex-con, that he couldn't hire him because the policy of the company in New York is that they do not hire ex-cons. That is one of the bad features that's going on. This guy wrote this manager who wrote a letter to the company and said that he would personally accept responsibility for this man because he was sure that he would make good. All the guy had done was make out a couple of bad checks and got sent to the penitentiary for it, came out and wanted to go back to work as a shoe clerk but because he'd made that mistake, even though he's paid his penalty, why he's taboo in a lot of places now. Then they wonder why these guys go out and sign more checks or steal more money.

One of the hardest things that I've found to do is to mind your own business when you're a square-john. As a criminal, in order to survive you have to know everything that's going on in the neighborhood and why they're doing it. Any action that's unusual, you investigate, because it might be policemen staked out or something like that. As a square-john, you just go on about your business. And I found that it was so hard, and still is, to ignore what other people are doing, especially if it's something that's unusual.

Another thing that's extremely hard to do is to get accustomed to a square-john girl. Now I know several thieves that have married square-john girls and they test their ability to handle a girl because they think altogether differently, not just as a man and a woman, but they think altogether differently. I prefer, frankly, to be with a rounder type of girl, a girl that works in a bar or is a barmaid, or a dice girl, something on that order, that's a rounder—shoplifter, prostitute, something like that. When an ex-thief lives with a prostitute, it doesn't necessarily mean that he's a pimp; he might just live with her for the companionship and some of them make very good wives, believe me.

I've known girls who wouldn't dream of going out with anybody except on business and they keep a very good home, are immaculate in their body, which is a hell of a lot more than I can say for a lot of square-john girls I've gone out with. Of course, I don't say that they're all that way, I just say that there are a lot of them that are that way, that are sloppy and cryin'. Most of the rounder type girls have been through the mill. It's like right now I'm going with a square-john girl and everytime I accidently say a swear word, why she corrects me about it. She knows all those words but she's always correcting me for saying something. If you're with a rounder girl, believe me, she says what she thinks and if she's going to swear, she says swear words and she knows them all and I guess that's one of the reasons so many of us guys like to be with a rounder type of girl. It seems like the square-john girl is trying to impress you or something and a rounder girl is just natural, just herself, that's all. You respect her for what she is and that's all there is to it. If you don't like her, well, go on about your business. I like that better than I do this "puttin' it on for me" business.

Another thing about the rounder girl is that she thinks the same way a thief does, in black and white. She's either with you or not with you, and if she's with you she's with you all the way and if she's not with you, well, that's it; she just backs off, gets away from you. She might have an affair with you but you definitely have an understanding that that's all it is, an affair; it's not going any further and it's just satisfying a sexual desire, that's all. But once she moves in with you, that's it. You're just as married as if you've been before every minister and priest in town and bought all the licenses there is to buy.

Once the adjustment sets in after an approximately ninety-day period, that's when it's the roughest for a guy coming out of the joint trying to get rehabilitated. He tries to understand everything and do everything at one time. Consequently he's tryin' to do his job and get rehabilitated at the same time and it can't be done very easy so he gets nervous, irritable, and he's tired all the time mentally, maybe not physically, but mentally he's tired all the time.

Nothing seems to go right. He don't understand his old lady unless she is that type of girl that's understanding and goes along with him, which a great many of them aren't; they don't realize that he's going through a change of life so to speak. So they expect the same thing from him that they would from some other guy and he can't produce right now. He's got to get adjusted first.

Some guys get adjusted in a very short period. Me—it took me approximately two years to get adjusted. Other guys never get adjusted. I know guys that's workin', that have worked ten years, and they're not adjusted properly, but by the same token I know guys that have come out of the joint that have done as much time as I have, been a thief as long as I have, and they get adjusted right now just as easy as could be and go right down on the line. A different type of person, I guess, adjusts differently.

I'm thinkin' of one guy in particular in Portland that I was in the joint with. We used to talk about going straight and he came out and went straight too and he never had any tiny bit of problem with it. He just took it all in stride and went right on down the line. Course he wasn't married at the time he came out and he met this girl afterwards—incidentally, she's a square-john girl—and if he didn't have a great deal of patience why his marriage would never work because she's always so afraid that he's goin' to get involved with somebody or do something and that's the best way to chase a guy back to it normally. But in his case why he's stronger than she is mentally and so he just goes along with it and pays no attention to what she thinks or says and knows that he's going to go straight and that's all there is to it. He went to work right away when he got out and adjusted very easily, likes his home life, but he's still very happy when some thief calls him on the phone or talks to him—that he misses: the old pals, friends he had.

You've got to remember that there was nothing bad about our associations on the other side of the fence—it was what the association led to, and that was penitentiaries. But for the people themselves, why we were all happy to know one another and to be associated with one another and perfectly happy in that society, and sometimes I think that they should allow us to associate more today and I think more guys would get straightened around. Like they should have a halfway house up here where they've got about fifty guys in it, and these guys are all ex-cons and they associate and talk to one another at night about different friends and different scores they've got and stuff like that and they get along fine; in the daytime they work. And

there's nothing wrong in that because if they're going to become criminals again, they're going to become criminals, that's all there is to it.

Politically appointing the warden of an institution or the parole
board for a state is way out of bounds. It's outrageous. Those people
should be picked for their ability. We have a few wardens in the country that are picked by examinations, but the majority of them, you'll
find, your chief of police, your wardens, your parole boards, are all
political plums and they have no experience whatsoever in handling
convicts prior to their going on the board and no background at all in
sociology. I think that we should have psychiatrists and psychologists
on this parole board, also in an institution.

When a man comes in the institution he should be given an examination by those people, given tests by those people, as soon as he gets
in the institution, before he's allowed to go to the yard and mix with
the other guys. Because once he gets out there he comes up with all
kinds of answers and some of them aren't very good answers. So it's
better that he be given an examination before he gets contaminated
by the other inmates. As I understand it, he can get tests—I believe
one of them is the Minnesota test, I'm not sure it's called that—so they
can find out what his aptitude is and assign him to a job where he's
got a chance to learn something that he'd be interested in, not just if
he's a carpenter put him in a plumbing shop. That's kind of on the order of the army I guess and it don't work out very well because they
eventually, in the army, put them back in the department where
they're best fitted.

In the institution, why hell, you just go out to the line and where
they happen to need a man, well, that's where they assign you. They
don't pay no attention to anything in your background or anything like
that. They don't care about anything like that. If you're a doctor you're liable to wind up in the carpenter's shop and that's very
common.

As far as this parole business is concerned, that's a lot of hooey.
That never cured any of these guys; you go down once a month and
make a report to a parole officer. How the hell are they going to reha-
bilitate anybody? These parole officers should be used to get jobs for
these guys.

They've got a long time ahead of 'em before they have to find a job
for a man and they know, we'll say three or four months ahead; why
they can look for a job that a man's best fitted at and when he comes
out we'll put him on that job. And do away with such things as halfway houses and stuff like that; they're not needed.

What this guy has to get is his self-respect back and the only way he's going to get it is to get on a job that he knows he can do right from the minute he starts that job. And he'll do all right. If he's going to go straight, he'll go straight and he'll go straight a heck of a lot quicker if he knows that he's going to a job that he understands, that he's learned in an institution and a job that he likes, a job he's fitted for, rather than come out and the parole officer tells him, "All right, you've got one day, two days, to get a job," and the guy don't know where to start; he's scared and everything else. That's not helpin' these guys.

These guys got to have help; they've got to be led by the hand for a little bit. What's wrong with our system today is they throw 'em on the street with a few bucks and that's all there is to it. Matter of fact, I've been told that there's a fund in the parole office to help guys on parole and one day I was talking to a parole officer and I wanted to borrow a couple of hundred dollars to buy a car, which I needed, and he told me that he'd been in the parole office for five years, I believe it was, and he had never heard of anybody being able to borrow any money out of this fund yet, which indicates to me that the fund has probably long ceased to exist, except in name only.

Now when I talk about jobs and things like that for these excons, I don't have reference to alcoholics and narcotics users because they're a special breed. I don't want to say nothing bad about 'em but I think they should be handled differently than you handle the average criminal comin' out of the institution. The average criminal is capable of going to work as soon as he comes out and staying on the job if he wants to. An alcoholic is liable to fall off the wagon at night—so is a narcotic user—and slip back down the grade so I do think that they need some kind of supervision until they get straightened out. Half-way houses or something on that order would be a good thing for them. But for the average criminal comin' out of an institution, the quicker you put him to work at something that he likes, the better off he's going to be and where else should you take and try and find out what he likes and what he should be than in an institution where he's laying there like a vegetable for three years and a half, or something like that, doing nothing.

One of the bad features that creates so much animosity between the inmates and guards in an institution is that the guards are all of a low-class workingman. The pay is very low, and their life is in danger all the time so they don't draw a very good type of man. That's what makes the inmates find that they're easy to bribe; they trade 'em leather goods, stuff that they've made, wallets, bags, women's handbags, and stuff like that for narcotics that friends of theirs slip to the guard and then the guard packs into them. They very seldom will bring a pistol because they're afraid there to have one in the institution for fear that they'll be the one to get shot with it but they'll do most anything else for money because they're underpaid. So you don't draw a very good class of man to an institution. The warden is about the only job, the warden and deputy warden, they're about the only two jobs that really draw any type of money. Even the doctor is underpaid in those institutions.

Most of these guards are about half afraid to start. So they're like a dog that bites you; why he don't really want to bite you but you startle him and scare him; why he'll bite in what he thinks is self-defense. Well that's the same way with these guards. They get involved with brutality not so much because they're brutal as the fact that they're half scared and three or four of them will get together and gang up on a guy and they get carried away and give him a terrific beating and pretty soon why they're brutal on their own.

I've seen a lot of brutality in institutions, but I've never let it plug my mind up. When I get away from it I forget it and that's all there is to it. But a lot of guys go out of those institutions and they hate the guards so bad that they try to get revenge when they get out for the beatings or something like that that they got. There was a riot in that Southern penitentiary the other day; well there's your brutality right there. They shot down into the yard and they killed those seven cons and wounded several dozen more of them when it was not necessary to do so but the Southern prisons are still that way. They're the only ones left that are that way. Northern prisons are pretty cold-blooded but they're not brutal anymore like they used to be. They're brutal to a few of them, the hard-core inmates that come in there with brutality on their mind, and they indicate it and show it and bring it out; why the officials retaliate. But the average guy can go in most joints today on the West Coast and all the Northern states and do time and do his own time without any trouble at all.

I know if I were to hate for all the beatings I've got in my life from policemen and institutions that I would have been dead a long time ago because I would have killed somebody. But I never let it bother me; I kind of considered the source and went on about my business.

One thing I have found, and there is no difference between a criminal and an alcoholic or a narcotics user in this respect: The danger of returning to the old life *always is there*. I know sometimes I get depressed and feelin' real bad and I don't understand why I'm going straight, I can't see any sense to it whatsoever. I made good money, I lived good, and I survived the penitentiary. That was a part of my crime. So I don't know what I'm doing on this side of the fence.

Now that doesn't last very long but it does come up occasionally and I've talked to other guys and they tell me the same thing. Every once in a while the temptation is there. I guess it's just that some of us are just strong enough to resist, I really don't know. We don't go back, but the temptation comes up. An illustration is: a while back when I had these two broken fingers and was feelin' pretty low about the fact that I was using up my savings to get by, two guys came to me that used to be partners of mine and they had a good score and they wanted me to go with them on it, offered me an equal share and we figured about $20,000 would be what the score would run and that's just what it ran. They went and got it just the way it was planned and everything and it was a really easy score. I came home after talkin' to them. I sat and thought and thought and I didn't talk to anybody; I wouldn't let nobody influence me. I decided that I'd have to decide this for myself. I almost called a professor friend of mine to ask his advice. But I said, "No, there's nobody that can help but myself." So I decided no, I didn't want nothing to do with it. Well these guys thought I was crazy when I told them, "No, I guess I'd better not get involved." I tried to give them an explanation and they just looked at me like I had rocks in my head, which maybe I have, I'm not quite sure.

Incidentally, both of these guys are in jail now but on a different charge and the lawyer will probably get all the money. But the point is they did successfully accomplish this one caper, got away with the money, divided it and everything, and I would've had $6,000–$7,000 from my end and could have done what I want with it and quit. But the only thing in my mind is would I have quit?

I doubt it. I'd be just like the alcoholic or the narcotics user. I'd have gotten a taste of it in my blood and back we'd go again and I can't stand that so I have to abstain altogether. It's black and white, you either do or you don't. There's no halfway about it.

I know guys that do take and monkey around, do a little bit of stealin' once in a while and work too and they have strength enough evidently to do it. Course they'll eventually get caught. But I haven't got that kind of strength. I either have to steal or be a square-john and I've made up my mind to be a square-john and so I am one.

This story I have been told; I don't know whether it's true or not but I can believe it. That in the old days there was a law and that it was kept on the books because nobody ever bothered to change it for many years. It was only changed in recent years when somebody demanded that they be given what the law said. The old law read that a man that was released from the penitentiary would be given a horse and a bundle of kindling wood, and that law had never been changed in all these years. It's a real old law.

By the same token laws that we have today that say a man will be given $40 or $50 when he gets out are just as outdated as that horse and bundle of kindling law was. What a man has to have today is some place to stay, something he can't spend right away because the first thing he's goin' to do is go get a girl and a few drinks and that's the end of his $40 or $50 right there. Then he's going to start worrying as to how he's gonna live; well he has no alternative but to steal.

Who's he going to get money from? There's nobody gonna give him money, nobody gonna give him a place to stay. That's where these halfway houses are coming in right now but they still don't fulfill the purpose. The thing is that the man should be given some place to stay where he can repay, a hotel or something like that where he'd be given a month's rent; and then he can repay that rent out of his wages that he earns. He should be given a job as soon as he gets out, not be forced to go hunt for a job.

Now when I say the parole officers should be changed to where they are not parole officers but people who help to find jobs for these guys, why I don't mean that they shouldn't have any supervision over the man; I mean their main duty should be to find a job. Now the rules, or the law, reads—I don't know which you'd want to call it or which it really is—that the parole officer visit each one of his men on his agenda once a month at his home so he can see what kind of place he's living in and so forth. Now he has all this workin' during the day to take care of—goin' to courts and stuff like that on parole violations and all those things, investigating—and every parole officer here in Seattle has at least a hundred cases. Now if he's got a minimum of a hundred cases, how in the hell is he going to take and visit all of these hundred cases once a month? That means he'd have to make three stops a night. Now he don't get paid for that night work, he don't get any overtime. He just gets paid for eight hours in the daytime and that's all. And it's part of his job to investigate these guys and a lot of them are workin' so he can't investigate 'em until night time so consequently he works at night too.

So actually that's a bad breakdown in your parole system right there. If people would get these guys a job when they get out and put them to work right away, a decent paying job, why then they would change this situation completely. We wouldn't have the muddle we've got now where these cons have no place to go to except back to their old stomping grounds, their friends that got out ahead of them from the penitentiary. If they had a job they would be so tired at night that they would go to bed. Maybe on the weekend they'd get a few drinks in or something like that but by that time they'd have gotten a week's work under their belt.

When I used to steal why we'd go and visit other thieves, my old lady and I, and we'd visit some other thief and his old lady and maybe there'd be six people then, and we'd sit up there and cut up what we call "old-touches"—that's a phrase for discussing old capers, "cuttin' up touches"—and we would get a great kick out of it. We'd go all through the old scores and discuss the ins and outs of it, the trouble we had with the safe or somebody asleep or in the joint or a means of entry or outrageous things that we found and things like that. And I can't honestly say that I have found anything to laugh about since I became a square-john. Everything's been so serious where I used to laugh a lot. I laughed when I fooled the bulls; I laughed when I pulled a good caper; I'd laugh when I'd sit with friends of mine and talk and I was happy go lucky. But since I turned a square-john why it's been all serious. It's been fightin' to understand and do like they do and I don't know.

I went out to the University of Washington to the employment office and filed for a job. A professor I know called them earlier and told them I was coming down because a professor does have a certain amount of influence there. I had insisted that he tell them about my past record. So I had a three hour interview with this counselor or whatever you call 'em, pertaining to a job. Fifteen minutes about the job and two hours and forty-five minutes answering questions about safes and about stealing. You don't realize how weary I grow of that. I insist on telling these people that I am an ex-criminal and they seem to be very intrigued by it, I don't know why.

They arrest men and send them to Walla Walla, which is clear over on the other side of the state, and want no part of them; they don't want to be seen with them or associated with them. But the first opportunity they get, why they want to know all about it. I don't dig it man, I just don't dig it.

I went all through this a thousand times now that they want to know all about me. How did I open a safe, not from the standpoint of wanting to open one themselves, but they don't understand how a man can open a safe without the combination. And I try to explain to them that I'm a destroyer, that I open a safe in whatever manner or means there is, that I make no attempt to burglarize a safe by a method so that the safe is preserved, I don't care about that; all I want is that money that's inside so I'll either burn, punch it, peel it or in some manner open it. I'm gonna open it all right.

A new era is coming in parole work and that is to utilize ex-cons as counselors and things like that. These PhDs and masters aren't the only ones that can counsel ex-cons and I know it's coming about. I know that in the near future it'll be a big thing. And unfortunately I'm just a little bit ahead of my time and I'm having' a *sad* time of it.

I know there is a place and it's like casin' a building; there's four walls, the roof, and the floor and there's a hole in that building someplace and there's a hole in this for breaking into counseling someplace but where I don't know. I sit here and think for hours at a time all by myself trying to think how I can get into this counseling and I can't think of an answer. I have several people who are willing to go to bat for me, who are willing to help me. I have innumerable people who want me to work but who do not have funds to pay me a salary—parole officers, the county, counselors want me, the D.V.R. [Department of Vocational Rehabilitation] wants me but they have no funds to pay me. Everybody wants me, there's two or three ministers that want me but they have nothing to pay me any room rent and food money. Of course, I can always go back to openin' safes at night and work as a counselor in the day time and that would keep me up to date.

In reference to these political plums like parole officers, parole board members, things like that, wardens and chief of police, let me illustrate one case that I know of for sure. A man was appointed to the Washington State Parole Board and had no qualifications whatsoever. I tended bar with him years ago, and after we quit tendin' bar he got some political strength and became sheriff. It was a known fact that he would take money at anytime. Quite recently he was appointed to the parole board by the governor as one of his last appointments: it made the present governor very unhappy about it. But quite recently we had a great deal of trouble here on the rackets controlled by one organization in the county and one of the guys that owned a tavern out here hollered "Bull" and got up and testified that he couldn't operate unless he took his machines from these people and a few other things like that. This guy who is a parole board member, mind you, was a front man for this organization that owned all the machines. He was temporarily suspended from the parole board when it came out in the paper about it and then later reinstated by the present governor, which I don't quite understand because I thought the governor wanted to get rid of him originally. He had a golden opportunity when it was a known fact by even a layman reading the papers that this guy was a front man for these people [the racketeers].

Kennedy [Robert] was shot last night and I read about it in the paper this morning, also that Johnson made the comment that he was going to assign bodyguards to all the men who were campaigning for the President's position. My estimation: why didn't he do this before? They knew there was a potential danger, especially to Kennedy, and in my own personal opinion why if McCarthy would have been nominated in California last night it'd have been him that would have been shot.

To show you how hard it is to become a square-john and do the things that you know will help why I had an interview the other day on this job [to counsel ex-convicts] and I can tell from talking to the guy that interviewed me that they wanted very badly to punch a hole in this wall surrounding an ex-con but everybody's afraid to undertake it for fear that it'll fall on its face. Well supposing it does fall on its face? There's no harm done. Everything falls on its face—in school when you teach, why everything you teach isn't absolutely correct; you know that and I know that. In the books that are written there's things that are not correct and not true so what is the difference here? It's like this police lieutenant that I talked to said, "Well they've tried everything else so now why don't they try this ex-con bit and see if it don't help."

I wanted to be put in group therapy. I talked to the assistant director about it and I said, "Well I'd like to be put in group therapy if I go to work and on my own time I'll do it, in the evenings, once a week or somethin' like that," and he said, "Well that's entirely up to you if you do that, I have regular office hours and I keep 'em." He said, "Anybody that wants to consult me has to consult with me during those working hours." Well that's silly. When you're a counselor of a bunch of people, like these potential criminals and things like that, they don't get in trouble eight hours a day. They're potentially in trouble twenty-four hours a day. They have to have a phone where they can contact you or see you and talk to you when times get rough for them mentally, like in the middle of the night, so they can call you up and talk to you in a little bit. I don't dig this at all, the way it's goin', but it is an opportunity for me to get my foot in the door if I do get it. I haven't got it yet. If I do get it it's an opportunity for me to get my foot in the door and then I will go from there. If I can handle it; I don't know as yet if I can handle it or not, and I don't know if I can keep my mouth shut at the right times; I'm not much of a politician.

I've put this whole bit down to one thing and that is there are a great many people interested in it but they're all pulling in different directions so consequently they're not accomplishing a great deal. Each one's in a little puddle by himself. All these puddles together would make a pretty good sized lake, I think, and we'd accomplish something then.

I was just thinking about an old box man I know in a joint down in New Orleans. I was sitting here the other night listening to some jazz music and thinking, Jesus, I'd like to see Kenny and see how he was doing down there. I still feel that way about it. But I found out I can't go on and steal and be a square-john too. So I got to make up my mind, so I'm a square-john now.

There've got to be some drastic changes made and it's with the youngsters out there. Somebody's got to start helping these kids. I talk to these kids sometimes myself; I don't know what the hell they're thinking about. I mean I can understand stealing for profit, I think everyone can understand that; that makes sense, you're at least making a profit out of it. But I mean, stealing these cars and run 'em till they run out of gas, what's that?

They're down there shooting narcotics. A friend of mine, a stickup man, just came in here from Los Angeles a while back and I went and found a connection for him up on Jackson and he went up there and where one pot, a spoon of stuff—narcotics—would usually satisfy him, you know, take care of his habit, he had to buy five of 'em in there and there were some kids in there that bought one spoon and were all knocked out from it. You see, it's in their minds. That's half of this stuff, this narcotics and stuff like that those kids are taking; it's in their minds. It's not a real habit.

Putting people in institutions is no answer. You can't take somebody off the street like that and just flat lock 'em up, I mean it's not a answer. I went through that. All it did is make me say well to hell with ya. I'll tear your town up next time for a reason. So I did. They all think that.

I don't know why I'm going straight. Here I'm without a job and it's a little rough, and I still feel the same way. It's just like I was talking with a psychiatrist that I see all the time, and I told him, "Man, this is silly; heck, I can go out here and in one night make enough to carry me for six months, you know." He was mad at me.

I wish I knew why I retired. I really wish I knew, because these guys come in all the time that I see that I know and they're out here enjoying themselves, they got a pocket full of money; and, believe me, there's nothing harder in the world to understand than square-john people. I understand my people—they're a bunch of bums. I know it and they know it, but I don't understand square-johns.

9

The Journey's End

"The wise guy winds up sleeping in the Hoosier's Barn."

I've worked here in Seattle in various jobs. One of them was working for a trucking outfit. I took a contract for them loading box cars. That's when I had a coronary heart attack. I didn't know at the time that I had it until I went to the hospital for an operation and they told me that I had had a heart attack in such and such a month. They assigned a specialist to me and he told me I couldn't walk upstairs, that I had to quit smoking and all kinds of crap.

I went back out to the hotel where I was living; I lived on the third floor incidently. I walked up the stairs, thought it over, went down to the basement and there was a concrete weight there that must have weighed three hundred pounds. I could just barely move it. It had a piece of pipe in it. I grabbed ahold of this to see if I was an invalid or if I was well. I lifted it and nothing happened. I didn't die or nothing. So I decided that I didn't have to go through all of what the doctor told me, but that I could do anything that I wanted to do. Six months later I went down and saw this doctor and told him what I had done. He said that he expected such a thing from me.

I couldn't get adjusted properly. I still thought in black and white. There was no grey, perhaps, or maybe. You do or you don't, that's all there was to it. No in-betweens of any kind. You liked a person or you didn't like him. I still thought as a criminal. A friend of mine persuaded me to go up and see the psychiatrist. I went up and saw him. I took treatments from him for a couple of years. Since then I have become a good friend of his.

The psychiatrist has never made a flat statement concerning why I went straight; neither has he said why I went crooked. I think he knows more why I went crooked than why I went straight. He has

129

made the statement that he believes that this training that I had in the institution did have an influence on my going straight. This is the only answer I ever could come up with concerning why I went straight. The life term of a safe cracker is rather long because you always use a younger man to do all the heavy work. All you have to use is your experience. That's what I could be doing today.

After I quit this trucking company, I went to a school that the Department of Vocational Rehabilitation sent me to. But I am not much of a reader and school is something that I don't understand too much. You show me something and I can assimilate that. But to sit down and read about it is extremely hard for me to do. I went to this school through its duration. When I came out I really didn't know my job. Thus, I never took it up. Someone offered to send me to another school, but I couldn't see the difference between one school and another as far as benefiting me.

One day I was talking to a friend and I told him that I felt that I owed an obligation to somebody, I really didn't know who. I wanted to help. That was when I met this professor [Bill Chambliss]. It's the first time to my knowledge that I have ever talked to a professor of a university. I'll be frank; when he first started talking I didn't know what the hell he was talking about. It wasn't until he got a little better acquainted with me and could come down to my level and talk my language that I could understand him. I had the same trouble today. I was out at the university arranging for a seminar. I talked to another professor. He talks way over my head. I guess I will have to educate him too. He is an extremely nice man.

I am dumbfounded to this day that this professor persuaded me to get up in front of a class and talk to them as we did that first time. After I talked to him a little bit, I said, boy I don't understand this guy. His thoughts and his outlook shook me up. I couldn't understand it. I had never come in contact with anyone like him before or any other professor. I went down and saw a friend of mine who was on the FBI. I asked him if there was a list of known Communists or people with Communist leanings. He said yes. I gave him the professor's name and asked him if he would look it up. A couple of days later he called me and I went down and had coffee with him. Of course that was against all rules and regulations for him to look that up and release that information. He wouldn't even tell me on the telephone. He told me no, that he was not a Communist and had no Communist leanings. This relieved my mind. I haven't anything against a Communist. But I don't want to be one so I don't see any reason for associating with one. Liking the professor, I didn't want him to be one. I guess I wanted him to be like me.

I got interested in the kids out at school. I saw how much benefit they could be toward the axe I had to grind pertaining to teaching these guys a trade in the institution. Not after they get out. These halfway houses are outrageous. They are using them all over the country and they are getting more of them everyday. They are a crutch. The man should be taught the trade before he gets out of the institution and when he is released from the institution he should be able to go right to work at his trade.

After I found out that I was going to be all right I went up to a guy who has since become a very good friend of mine. I went to work for him contract painting, painting on the outside of buildings. I did all the outside painting off a scaffold for him. We got along fine, but he had a partner who was always trying to take advantage of everybody. I had two or three beefs with his partner so I finally quit.

I was still painting when I met a girl who was a whore. She was using narcotics. She was in pretty bad shape. I think I got acquainted with her through a hype friend of mine. This girl told me that she wanted to quit narcotics. So I told her that I would help her. She had an apartment up on Capitol Hill. I was working long hours because this was contract painting that I was doing. I told her that anytime that she had problems or couldn't sleep to call me. She used to pick outrageous hours, like two and three o'clock in the morning, to call me. I would have to sit there patiently for two hours and listen to her. Finally I went up to see her and I asked her if she really did want to quit. She said yes. I told her that I would move in with her. I wasn't going to be her pimp but I would just move in with her.

We got another apartment with two bedrooms. I tried to explain to her one day about the seminars [at the university]. She said I was a do-gooder, which was a slanderous term to her. She didn't like it. I guess she wanted me to be a criminal. She knew all about me before I moved in. I went to this psychiatrist friend of mine and told him that she wanted to get off. He prescribed some medicine that would help to carry her.

A hype today, although it costs him a lot of money to support his habit, really doesn't have a bad habit. That stuff has been cut so many times that by the time they get it, there is really no strength left in it. The doctor and I talked this over and we decided to try a real mild sedative and see if that wouldn't take her off. Well it did. I went on working. She would never go to bed until three or four o'clock in the morning and I would get up at five or six o'clock in the morning. Consequently, I would have to go to bed pretty early. She didn't mind because she would sit up and watch TV. I insisted that she take Sunday off every week so that we could go someplace. I got her out of debt, she was badly in debt. I bought a car. She couldn't stand that high living I guess because she started using narcotics again.

I just don't think those people can be cured. Nobody seems to believe it except this outfit that is trying to cure them. They have a problem. The problem is still there, whether they are using the narcotics or not.

By the same token, I have the same problem too. I quite often think about crime. I wonder what I'm doing by going straight. That I'm a fool and things like that. But the temptation isn't great, an idle thought actually.

Well Judy returned to narcotics. Then she began to shoot goofballs and things like that when she couldn't steal or cheat enough from me. I kept track of all the money. She couldn't afford to have it so she started shooting goofballs. That really did upset the family. There was nothing left. I took her up to the psychiatrist. He talked to her for three straight hours. When he was through he said to me that the best thing I could do was to get away from her. He is a very devout Catholic and he is a very strong believer in trying to help anybody. So I did; I had that much respect for him that I immediately got away from her. I occasionally see her downtown. I think she blames me for her using narcotics, I don't know.

After I broke up with Judy I was confused because basically I want a home. I'm too old for children now in any form, they get on my nerves. After I left her I was pretty badly upset for a long time. Not particularly about her but the fact that she was a woman. I refused to have anything to do with any other girl.

Then they persuaded me to go out to pier 91; that's a navy pier. I went out there to work. In the meantime this seminar had been dropped. I didn't feel like talking to the classes so I terminated that. The professor who first got me started out there had moved away. I worked at pier 91 for a year and a half as a rigger and a forklift operator. I got along fine. Seventy-five percent of the men employed there are Negroes. I got to learn quite a bit about them that I never knew before because I had never been in close contact with them. Then I broke two fingers on my hand so I quit. I had been toying with the idea of becoming a counselor for ex-cons for a long time.

I am going out to a place called Providence Heights. I am going to talk to some sisters out there. This is one thing I have to admit, being a Catholic, but the priests that we get in an institution are usually the outcasts. They don't fit into any parish properly so they ship them to an institution. Some of them are terrible. My contention is that the sisters could do more good in an institution then the priests do. The sisters are more sincere. I don't want to say that the priests are bad, but I want to give the sisters more credit for being more sincere than the priests are. I am going out to these sisters and tell them they can be of more benefit than by just being school teachers. Nurses and school teachers, that's all they do. They get masters and PhDs right out at the University of Washington. Then they are put in some elementary school. They have too much ability for that.

An acquaintance of mine came up from Portland and told me that he wanted to go to work in Seattle. He asked me if I could help him out financially, which I couldn't because I had recently been ill. I had acquired a large hospital bill. He asked me if he could call me that night and I said yes. At about two in the morning he called me and asked me to come down to the lobby. He didn't know that there was a policeman on the beat there who was more or less hiding out between his rounds. He was sitting there without his uniform on reading the paper. He saw this fellow come in with a large paper sack under his coat, which was kinda stupid. He came back and knocked on my door. I let him in. He dumped the contents of this bag on my bed. It contained $14,000 in paper and silver. I made the comment at the time, "penitentiary here I come," because I knew that he had stolen the money. His idea was to give me some money, which is quite common among criminals.

This policeman who saw him come in with this bag under his coat was aware of my background. He came back and knocked on the door. I, without any thought at all, opened the door. Here was all this money on the bed. The officer arrested us both, which he had no choice.

I went down to the station and they held me for eight days, four days in the city jail and four days in the county jail, before they released me. At that time they threatened to try me as an accessory to this man's crime. They solved the crime the next day and found out where he got the money. I almost went to the penitentiary because I was eligible as a perpetual criminal and I almost went for the rest of my life. I was released, the whole thing was kind of outrageous, but they could have done it. Legally they could have done it very easily.

I see criminals all the time. They don't try to get me to work with them; they just ask me if I would like to. I was a pretty good thief, a conscientious one. I worked hard at it when I did work at it. They will try to get me to go with them because they know I will case a joint real well before I go on it. I've been tempted to join them innumerable times. It's a much simpler and easier life. I was raised up in it, grew up in it and lived all my adult life in it. Like I said, I like those people that I worked with.

But living with square-johns is different. If I don't want to work to-night I don't see any reason why I have to go into a detailed explanation with the official out there. I just say that I don't feel like working and I lay off. But a square-john wants to get real complicated and have their wife call up and say that they are sick. You are much more your own boss when you are working as a thief. All thieves hate regimentation, which is something they have to accept when they go to a penitentiary. They all resent that very much. So, consequently, when the opportunity presents itself to get away from there they do.

Today I read about two guys who got knocked over for holding up a bank. I read that article several times and I just laughed. I can get up, go out, get a cup of coffee and walk in the sunshine. And what do those guys have? You can believe that I am very thankful to the people that I have had to help me. That's why I want to help too now. Without people helping me, not as a crutch but a little nudge here and there, I would never have made it.

What bothers me the most is how they can send a guy to the university and afterwards he can get a job as a counselor. He immediately begins to counsel young guys. Most of these guys don't know one thing about how these kids think. All they know is what they have read in the book. I know what these kids think. I know what they think twenty-four hours a day. I know the thoughts and words that they use all the time in the institution. That part of the institution doesn't change. I know these things and still I cannot get a job as a counselor's aid. Those kids don't know anything about this education. Like the other day I was talking to this counselor. He used this word motivation all the time. I don't even know what it means.

I just can't understand why there isn't a place for me somewhere. Quite often I think how crazy I am to go straight especially when these guys come through. A couple of guys I know made a real good string here up the country a while back and they say come in, and they just begged me; they had a little trouble with this box and they knew they would have, and they knew I knew how to take it and they begged me and told me they'd give me any part of the action if I'd get it because it had to be gotten right away while this money was still there. And I turned them down and neither one of them has talked to me since, because they flatly think I'm crazy.

I really don't know why I went straight. I just decided that after I got out. It wasn't fear of the law; it isn't fear of the penitentiary, 'cause I've sat down and thought it out very seriously, but I just had enough of it, that's all. The last time I was in the penitentiary I guess I was making a change then and didn't realize it.

I talk to young kids and our present system all over the world, I guess, is so far outmoded it's pathetic. For a progressive nation like this it is, especially. In Christ's time they was throwing guys in jail, lock them up and it didn't solve nothin'. All you're doin' today is you're paying taxes on joints like Shelton [Washington state's newest prison]. Why? There's no answer, they never have got an answer out of that.

I done time in penitentiaries when we used to hang the guys up by their thumbs and leave them there all day and used to, I mean, beat 'em. Really beat 'em. and they used to throw them in the black hole and leave them there for months, let them go crazy, hope they did and then never have to bother with them. That didn't stop them from stealing.

Guys get right out of that hole and I seen them beat up so bad that they have to put them in the hospital for two or three months, and soon as they come out of the hospital they'd walk right across the yard and sit down and start talking about crime. So obviously your system isn't very successful, and there's got to be a change someplace or something done about it. Locking these kids up isn't going to do any good.

If they took you out of circulation for three years, do you think you could come back and sit in with your old friends? You wouldn't have a chance. Do you know where you'd go? You'd go down and hunt up guys like me, because you'd just left me. We were congenial while we were in the penitentiary or the reformatory. Your friends would have progressed on, some had got married, some even have kids already, some are established in business and things like that. You have been taken out of circulation for that two, three years or whatever it is so you just can't fit back in there. You only have one place to go.

When they turn you out of those joints they just hand you a suit— they don't even give 'em a suit anymore. They just give 'em a jacket, pair of pants, tell 'em, "Go, man." Give you a few bucks. They usually try to send you to some town where you're not known and you go into strange surroundings, you are with strange people, you're confused and mixed up about the darn thing and there is nobody to help you. People take and condemn these guys—I'm not saying that they're right in stealing; I'm saying they need help.

A kid that's studying to be a doctor walked up to me downtown, after I talked to a class, and he was a real nice fellow, I liked him real well and he said, "You changed my perspective," I think the word is. That's one good thing about having only a third-grade education; I always say "I don't understand." I changed his point of view just talking to him. I think that if somebody would have tried to help me when I was a kid, now when I look back and think it over, I think I would have gone straight a hell of a long time ago, a long time ago. I don't say all these kids are going to be helped but if I can talk to someone and someday you just help one guy, that's all I ask. It would make me feel real good.

I'm really not enthused in going up to talk to classes at the university and telling that I've been a thief even though I've got nothin' to be ashamed of. I never robbed any poor people or hurt any individual; I just robbed big companies, and I thought it was legitimate. If you had asked me, I would have told you at that time too. But I've got just one thought in mind and that's to help somebody. Somebody's got to change this system, not just throw a guy in the joint.

I've been on parole for five years and I went down and I've seen the parole officer and I got some of the most fabulous letters you ever saw written for me. They all were legitimate letters—no fakes. I went down and saw the parole officer and talked to him about it and he said, "Well, you got to pay, Harry," and I said, "What the hell did I do that five years in the penitentiary for? What am I paying now for? Now I'm supposed to be getting adjusted. You sweet people are supposed to help me. Instead you tell me, a hundred years ago guys were put on parole; you go on parole too.''

Kinda silly, ain't it? Suppose they taught you in the school here like they did a hundred years ago. You wouldn't get very far today, would you? That's the same way with us unless somebody helps those guys out, a few of 'em, not all of 'em; there's some pretty bad bastards in there, I'll tell you. Real bad ones that would shoot you in the back in a minute. Instead they are building joints for these sex criminals. Building special joints for them and putting them in there. Then they turn 'em out, six months or a year, and put 'em on parole and they go right back to bothering the little kids and stuff like that. And they lock some guy up for stealing a car or something and say "in you go" and keep him there for a long time. Nobody makes any attempt to help him out.

I know a lot of guys and a lot of kids in the joints that are going back to stealing and they don't no more want to steal than you guys want to steal. I've talked to 'em and I've caught 'em when they felt like talking and they wished they had someplace or something to go to when they got out. And they haven't; everybody's too busy and he's a criminal.

I have a sister and a while back I was talking to her about it and she's a hell of a good girl. She's all for me. I said, "But I don't understand it," and she said, "Well, they're afraid that you'll go back stealing." I said, "But I never stole off them people." I never hurt an individual in my life. That was a darn good answer she gave me. She's a "square-john"; she's a member of society. She don't give no thought about it and her brother has been involved all these years. But she don't give no thought about it; she said, "But the law'll take care of him—maybe he should be out—they'll let him out."

I considered stealing a legitimate business. I have absolutely no interest in what other people do. I really don't think whether it's legitimate or illegitimate; that's for the guy that does it to decide. You see, I've got enough problems. I'm finding going straight a hell of a hard row to hoe. I'm fifty-six years old and I'm starting in a racket that I know absolutely nothing about. I don't know why I quit stealing. I didn't stop because I'm afraid. I didn't quit because I'm getting old, because I have guys show up here once a week to ask me to go look at a box—oh, once a month I'd say. Ask me to go look at a box and help them plan it out. So I didn't change for any reason that I know of. I mean it gets me a little confused sometimes why I really did change. I just don't know.

Becoming a square-john is a great deal harder than becoming a thief. You are associating with the people you use to sell stuff to and do business with. They go around with a halo on their head all the time and you know that that halo doesn't belong there. But you have to condone it and put up with it. It's like the comment I made to this guy the other day, that I do not accept society, I tolerate it. I have to; everyone else accepts it. In order to go along with the parade I tolerate it, but that is all I do.

Postscript

A few days after Harry made the last of the tapes from which the materials in this book have been taken, he telephoned me long distance. I had left Seattle years earlier and had now settled in Santa Barbara, California. But we had kept in touch. I had recently gone to Seattle to see him. It was Friday evening:

> *Bill you know I've been trying to get a job as counselor with the probation department. And they say they want me real bad for the job but they have to get a special position from the city council. Mr. Johnson at the department said he got fabulous letters of recommendation for me and all that, but I don't know, Bill, they keep stalling me on the thing and I'm really getting more and more depressed. They said they'd know definitely by next Tuesday. And if it doesn't come through I'm going to leave for good.*

We talked a little about the job as counselor and what it would mean. Then I asked what he meant by leaving. Did he mean he would go back to opening safes?

> *No. I couldn't do that anymore. I mean I'll go to sleep and make sure I never wake up.*

I was shocked but not surprised. He had hinted earlier that if things didn't improve he would kill himself. I knew Harry well enough to know that these were not empty threats but statements of fact. I tried to argue with him:

> *Harry, you know how difficult it is to get people to accept the idea that an ex-thief would be a good counselor for guys on probation. You shouldn't get discouraged.*

Harry responded:

> *But that's not the problem. They want me real bad. They know I've worked with some guys just on my own in the hotel room and had really fabulous results.*

The conversation continued in that vein: I arguing that he had to keep trying, he signalling a mounting sense of despair:

> *Bill, if this doesn't come through there just isn't any reason to go on. There are only two people in the world I care about: my sister, who's real nice to me but she has her own family and doesn't want an ex-thief botherin' her, and you, and you're down in California. I live in this crummy hotel room; got no girl; a job as a janitor that I can't make it on. Why should I go on like this?*

The following Tuesday I called him back. The job at the probation department had not materialized. But he had decided I was right; he should keep trying and it was worth the effort. But a week later, on Tuesday morning, Harry's sister called:

> *This is Mrs._____, Harry King's sister. He was found dead this morning in his hotel room. He left you a letter but I thought you'd want to know before the letter came. Did he commit suicide? Yes. He had put all his hopes in the job with the probation department and when it didn't come through he was so depressed. The letter he wrote you was taken by the police. They said they'd send it on to you.*

I turned on the tape recorder beside my desk, which had on it the last tape Harry would ever make. I listened to the tape again to hear Harry say "Bill, I'd like to make a tape on rehabilitation. I don't know if it will be of any use in the book but I want to make it anyway because it's been on my mind a lot lately." My wife Lou came into my study and cried with me knowing without being told the message brought by the telephone call.

The letter Harry left for me was mailed within a week. The police had opened the letter and written on the outside of the envelope "Exhibit 12417 Item 4." The letter was characteristically short and to the point:

> Dear Bill,
> By the time you receive this I will be dead and I want you to know that what I said on the phone the other nite I meant please don't think badly of

me for being a coward—I just don't want to go on this way any more. So thank for everything and tell Lou and the kids goodbye for me.

Harry

P.S. Anything I get from the book I would appreciate it if you would send it to my sister who I owe some money to. Thanks.

Commentary

Notes on Professional Theft, Law and Society

Every society has many living worlds that exist side by side in silence. The world that is visible to most people is their life; it is depicted albeit distorted in the mass media and it is assumed in conversation and nuance. The invisible worlds are available to fewer people. Those are the world of the ghetto, skid row, the night people and those on the fringe of "legitimacy." The invisible world is every bit as much a part of society as is the visible one. In fact, the invisible world is a crucial ingredient in society's fabric. No society could maintain its particular form if it did not have both worlds. If we are to understand society we must grasp the features of the invisible as well as we grasp those of the visible.

Grasping the invisible is almost a contradiction in terms. Occasionally, representatives of the two worlds get together and form an alliance. Then each is afforded an opportunity to see the other's world. This is what happened when I met and became friends with Harry King. Through him I discovered the invisible world of professional theft.

This discovery of professional theft is a curious thing. Every few years a book will emerge depicting professional theft as though it had just been discovered for the first time. Invariably the author of the book tells us that professional theft is dying and, like the cowboy and the hangman, is about to become extinct. On this assumption those who study (or should study) crime, juvenile delinquency and the law go back to sleep; go back to developing grand theoretical models about why kids become delinquent; go back to questioning inmates in penitentiaries or youths in college about their "deviancies" and assume that professional theft and "things like that" deserve a nod occasionally but are, after all, dying.

The blame for this narrowness of vision does not rest solely on those who read the books by professional thieves. As defenders of a way of life, thieves make very poor public relations men. For they too are constantly telling us that professional theft is dying out. Yet despite their pessimism thieves keep turning up. New types of theft are developed. New ways of opening safes emerge. When banks transfer their money to Brinks Armored Car Service then the thieves work out ways of robbing the armored cars. It may well be that it is the rapidly changing nature of professional theft that leads an old thief to always see the profession as dying. The old box man of the twenties who used nitroglycerin to open safes saw his craft vanishing when "kids" began punching and burning.

Despite these prognostications of gloom, the overwhelming evidence is that professional theft is no more dead today than it ever has been. There have always been a small cadre of devotees who consider themselves professional thieves; who plan their capers carefully; who develop their craft through apprenticeship and with planning. The number of men practicing the craft may never exceed a few thousand at any point in time. But though few in number they serve a variety of very useful purposes for the social order and so long as they provide a useful purpose they will remain. What useful purposes do professional thieves serve?

It is, as Harry says in Chapter Six, the police, the prosecuting attorneys, the fix and the judges who benefit most directly from professional theft. The thieves end up impoverished and in prison. It is only when that situation changes that we will see the death of professional theft. American society and American criminal law being what they are, we are not likely to see any profound changes in the near future.

The professional thief is an indispensable part of the legal system as it is constituted in America. The thief's role performs a host of services for the legal order that make it possible for law enforcers to perform the responsibilities of their roles much more efficiently and with much less strain than they could otherwise. For the police, the thief is willing to admit to the commission of numerous offenses that otherwise would go unsolved. Whether he committed them or not is irrelevant to the thief; the only relevant question the thief will ask is whether the police are willing to give him certain benefits in return.

For the prosecutor the thief provides a source of guilty pleas to a host of offenses which, if unresolved, would appear in the formal record to represent evidence of prosecutorial ineptness. That the police and the prosecutor must, in return for these bureaucratically useful admissions by the thief, provide him with license to steal is a fact rarely glimpsed by those looking "objectively" at the performance of officials who occupy key positions in the legal machinery.

The thief is also useful to the agencies of law enforcement in that if the agencies cooperate with him he will assist them in recovering stolen property when such recovery is essential for the smooth functioning of the legal agencies. Most thefts are from persons who are insured or who, for other reasons, are not too concerned about recovering the stolen items. For example, the cost of items shoplifted from supermarkets can be covered by adding a penny to the price of canned peas. But occasionally some items will be stolen from persons with considerable political and economic power in the community and the police will be judged by these persons according to their ability to recover the stolen items; indeed, their ability to recover the stolen items is of much greater importance in passing judgment on their efficiency than is the question of whether they apprehend the person that perpetuated the crime. If the police have an "understanding" with persons who receive and sell the stolen property and with the working professional thieves in the area then the chances of recovering a particular stolen item (or set of items) is much greater than if the police and the thieves are constantly at war.

Naturally, like any agreement between groups of persons, if the one group steps outside the tacitly approved limits of requesting favors, then the entire exchange system breaks down. Thus if the thief begins to commit thefts indiscriminately and "burns the town up," as Harry put it, then the police will invariably make an arrest and see that punishment is administered. Similarly, if the police begin insisting that one out of every three "marks" must be returned to the police then the thieves could be expected to balk and refuse to cooperate.

"No police force can operate without informers," Harry tells us. Having informers who are paid directly with police funds is inefficient, costly and expensive beyond what is easily justifiable to the politicians who control the purse strings. The obvious solution is to provide favors of immunity from arrest for those who are willing to inform. The local police are in an ideal position to develop such symbiotic relations with the thieves. As Harry points out, federal law enforcers must then depend on the local police to maximize their own access to informant information. In return, widespread corruption on the local level is overlooked.

Thieves are also in a position to embarrass and intimidate law enforcement agencies. The story told by Harry of dropping the opened safe on the lawn of the chief of detectives and calling the newspaper is a blatant illustration of how thieves can, in fact, "make life miserable" for law enforcers if they so choose. In addition, thieves can make public the fact that certain people in the political-legal structure of the community have accepted bribes. While such charges coming from a "known criminal" may not carry a great deal of weight, they will nonetheless serve as irritants to law enforcers and such situations will therefore be avoided whenever possible.

Thus we find the thief and law enforcement agencies entering into a symbiotic relationship in which each group aids the other for the mutual benefit of both. The "public" is unaware. Indeed, because many of the more important functions of the legal system can apparently be performed within the context of this relationship, when the relationship is solid, the "public" is satisfied that the job of enforcing the law is being carried out satisfactorily.

Professional thieves are also valuable to a host of other groups. They help insurance companies sell theft insurance. To be sure, if the thefts in a particular area are too frequent an insurance company is likely to put pressure on the police to find the thieves and incarcerate them. Without any thefts, however, companies would not have a market for their insurance at all. Like the law enforcement agencies, insurance companies need a useful level of theft within every community: a level that keeps businesses and the general population sufficiently alarmed that they will pay the premiums on their insurance but a level that is not so outlandishly high that the premiums charged in order to make a profit interfere with the insurance companies' ability to sell policies.

The manufacturers of safes are perhaps the most obvious private beneficiaries of the safecrackers' illegal practices. The "rip and tear" method of opening safes, which is the most common method, renders the safe unusable after the theft and therefore necessitates replacement.

There are still more important ways in which professional theft contributes to social order. The thief is, in fact, every bit as important to the structure of American society as is the corporation executive, the professor, the medical doctor, the lawyer and others.

The director of a large business enterprise is revered and his position at the top of the economic elite of the society is justified on the grounds that he contributes so much to the welfare of so many. His contribution may be partly charitable but mainly it is seen as stemming from the fact that he provides jobs for many people, that the director's business stimulates the economy and that he adds incentive for technological change and progress.

The professor is similarly given high status and high income. His contribution is seen as being one of contributing knowledge to the general progress of society and to educating the young.

The thief is disdained, maligned and punished. Yet by the same criteria that lead us to revere the businessman, the thief is a magnificent and proud example of capitalism at its very best. He makes jobs not only for people who make the safes he opens but for insurance companies. He makes jobs for lawyers, policemen, social workers, judges, prosecuting attorneys and, not the least of all, professors who write books about thieves, students who study them (and thereby stay a little longer from the already overly populated labor market), book publishers, book salesmen. Indeed, an entire industry thrives on the work of the thieves. And the thief contributes to technological advance: safes are made safer, locks are made more secure, innovations occur in the handling of money (notice the armored car and the entire industry that has grown up around this), ingenious devices are invented for the protection of stores, factories and homes.

There are other striking similarities between the thief and the most revered professions. The thief spends long and arduous hours learning his craft (just as businessmen, doctors and professors do); the thief also feels an obligation to pass on this information and train others.

The similarity goes even further; and perhaps it tells us a good deal about the political-economic structure in which we live. The thief shares with the businessman a commitment to violation of certain laws whenever necessary. He may be more willing to take risks (after all the thief loses only his freedom, not his social standing, when he goes to prison) than the businessman, but both engage in systematic violation of the law. For the thief these are the activities of theft in its many forms; for the businessman they are violations of the law such as misusing funds, embezzlement, disregarding antitrust laws, misusing child labor, ignoring safety regulations for factories and, of course, income tax evasion. But the principle remains the same; the thief and the businessman systematically and consistently violate the law.

The two also have in common an incredible immunity from criminal prosecution and for much the same reason. Like the businessman, the thief can provide many useful services for the law enforcement agents if his transgressions are overlooked. The businessman provides campaign funds for political officials, bribes, tips on smart investments, cooperation in mutually rewarding "investment opportunities." The thief provides untaxed income for those who help him and a host of essential information about thefts, thieves, whores, drug users, subversives and the like. The immunity enjoyed by the thief and the businessman, then, stems from the fact that both provide officials of the criminal justice apparatus with services and economic support, which they desire and need.

Less obviously, but no less importantly, the thief also serves as a smokescreen behind which all kinds of illegal and quasi-legal activities can be hidden. The presence of professional thieves committing crimes that can be publicized and have an intrinsically interesting flavor to them—such as elaborate con games, safecracking and armed robberies—provides law enforcement agencies with materials for creating public support for the police. This focusing of public attention on such crimes diverts attention from crimes of exploitation. It effectively dims perception of the highly selective nature of the law enforcement process. A community that is reminded that professional thieves are working in its midst cannot be expected to demand and insist that law enforcement agencies concentrate much of their energies on the crimes of the persons in political and economic power—such as violations of laws against discrimination in employment, illegal advertising or misleading claims about interest rates paid on installment purchases.

The presence of professional thieves also serves as a smokescreen that diverts attention away from organized crime activities in which police and political figures invariably enjoy substantial profits and have considerable investment. A citizenry that is constantly reminded of the presence of dope fiends, muggers, rapists, and even professional robbers, burglars, safecrackers and con men can be expected to respond rather nonchalantly to the apparently minor problems of widespread gambling, loansharking, labor racketeering and prostitution in their midst.

From the point of view of the welfare of the entire community, it may well be that paying attention to crimes of exploitation and corruption would in the long run serve the interests of the community to a much greater extent than does concentrating on crimes ordinarily committed by professional thieves. The symbiosis between organized crime and the legal system undermines the very heart of the democratic process, and the hostility of ghetto dwellers that culminates in riots and local revolutions might well be abated if the laws against discrimination and exploitation were enforced. But to enforce such laws would not be in the best interests of the law enforcement agencies. It is not "good administration" to enforce them. Were the prosecutor or the police to decide to enforce laws prohibiting false claims of interest in installment purchases, the business community would rise as a body and virtually impeach the law enforcers. Similarly, should the law enforcers enter into a campaign to rid a city of political graft and corruption tied to organized criminal syndicates, the persons at the pinnacles of political and economic power in the community would demand the heads of the law enforcers engaged in such "irresponsible and even scandalous behavior." It is simply "not good business" for law enforcement agencies to undertake the strict enforcement of these laws and, indeed, they rarely do.

The businessman is a hero; the thief is a villain. And in playing these roles each serves the interests of the established order. For the middle-class child the prospect of failure is embodied in the image of the villainous, pathetic thief. This image, then, is a motivating force for working toward success. The image of the heroic businessman, with all his prestige and obvious success, is also a motivating force. Furthermore, and this is equally important, the middle-class child finds the avenues to business relatively open and available; the avenues to becoming a thief are distant and difficult to imagine.

The world of the lower-class child is somewhat different. Thieves, bookmakers, derelicts, hustlers, con men *and failures* are omnipresent. This world is perceptible and real. It is, in the words of a fifteen-year-old junkie from the Milwaukee ghetto, "beautiful." The world of the businessman is remote and difficult to imagine. "Society"—the "square-john" society—may see the thief as the villain and the businessman as the hero but to lower-class youngsters the businessman is likely to be the *real* villain and thief. Their perception of the world is, in some respects, more realistic: they see everyone fighting for survival in a hostile world.

The established order is thus maintained. Lower-class youth do not make a revolution to overthrow the economic and political relations that exist: they strive, instead, to find their place in those relations, and their place is likely to be one for which the model of the thief is a useful vision. If they are capable and lucky they will become thieves. If they are less talented or less fortunate they become petty criminals or junkies or skid row derelicts. Just as not all middle-class youth will find their place among the economic elite but will have to settle instead for the modest rewards of rountine jobs in middle-level occupations, so most of the lower-class youth will have to settle for modest rewards from routine jobs on the fringes of both the professional thief's and the "square-john's" society. But the vision of the professional thief, likes the vision of the president of a corporation, is a useful image in the makeup of the world of the growing child, and it helps to maintain at least acquiescence if not outright support for things as they presently exist.

We find that the organization of law enforcement helps to create and sustain professional thieves, *not* deter or reduce their numbers. So it is not surprising that we find a host of laws and institutionalized law enforcement practices that serve to perpetuate the profession of theft. Indeed, the process of perpetuating the individual in crime is maximized at every point that he makes contact with the law.

If we want to understand the profession of theft we must, then, grasp this elemental feature of the role: professional theft contributes mightily to the society. It cannot be eliminated or altered by arresting and confining professional criminals. If we would change the profession of theft we would fight against all that is sacred in society; we would deny the wisdom of the society in creating and maintaining institutions, roles, and occupations that contribute to the maintenance of the present order. Making a revolution, we would become criminals ourselves.

The entire process of "becoming a thief" is as surely a matter of recruitment into socially necessary roles as is the process of becoming a doctor, a medicine man, or a guru. Once the thief is engaged in the professional, the legal machinery is so structured that he is virtually guaranteed an ongoing place in the world of crime. By becoming enmeshed in a set of interdependencies and commitments that are as difficult to break out of as those surrounding any other occupation in society, the "line of least resistance" for the thief is always more theft. For example, once the thief is arrested he must post bond. There is obviously only one way for the thief to obtain the money to pay the bail bondsman's fee and that is to steal the money. In addition, the professional thief knows that the safest and fastest way out of the "beef" is the "fix." And the fix will cost more money and will, then, cause more crime. Thus the system is perpetuated.

After a thief serves a prison sentence, he finds that the possibility of participation in the "square-john" society has been severely restricted. Policemen, suspecting him of returning to thievery, harass him and warn employers to "watch him." If, as in Harry's case, a policeman has a particularly strong dislike for the thief, he can put pressure on employers not to hire him. Insurance companies raise their premiums for businesses employing ex-convicts or refuse to insure them at all. Employers are reticent to hire ex-convicts regardless or their skills. Thus, the rite of passage back into "square-john" society is so structured that the thief invariably finds that the path of least resistance leads back to a life of theft. The profession of theft is thereby preserved and all the benefits of that role to society are guaranteed.

Every society has a differentiation of tasks and, in one way or another, these tasks become attached to certain positions. Medicine men, carpenters, doctors, professors and warriors are but a few of the almost infinite number of such positions. Societies also have their deviants. Typically we analyze society in ways that suggest that some of these tasks are sought and others avoided. There are a number of things that lead us to the inference that society encourages certain roles and discourages others, for example, the rewards attached to the roles. If a role carries with it a high level of general esteem, power, wealth and privilege, then we say those are things that encourage people to seek the role. If, on the other hand, persons who occupy certain roles are generally held in disrepute, punished for their actions, not allowed to share in the wealth of the society and kept from positions of power then we are prone to say that those positions are discouraged. One other criterion is frequently brought forth: if certain structural features of the society encourage and educate some individuals in various ways so that they are moved along the lines that appear inevitably to lead a particular role, then we are likely to say that that role is sought by the organization of the society, if not by its moral dictates.

When we are depicting society in these commonsense ways we, of course, leave out a great deal in order to make the picture we paint sensible. Thus we emphasize the advantageous features of a role when we want to underline the fact that it is a role of importance to the society. For example, we ignore the long hours, lack of privacy and incredible tension in the life of a doctor and stress instead the rewards of money, security and service. We point out, however, that the rewards are really necessary in order to get people to seek a position that does involve some disadvantages after all.

By contrast, when we speak of the thief's position we typically emphasize the undesirable features of it—the possibility of a prison sentence, the disruptive influence on a "normal" family life, the disrespect of the community likely to arise if the fact of being a thief is discovered. Again, we ignore some features of the position—in this case, the desirable ones. But we do add, parenthetically, in much the way we do when discussing doctors, that there are apparently a few incentives to being a thief after all. For example, to understand why some people do choose to be thieves, we might mention such things as the excitement and challenge as well as the economic incentives.

Because we use the same perspective for explaining the acceptance and commitment to the role of the thief as we do for the acceptance of and commitment to the more prestigious roles in the society, it is obvious that we should come to the same general conclusion: There are mechanisms, tendencies, structural characteristics, rewards and motivational sources that lead persons to be attracted to both roles.

Now, one may argue that what this suggests is that depictions of the way we go about getting people to become doctors, lawyers, and chiefs are erroneous. I don't think they are. But, at any rate, it seems accurate to say that the methods of motivating people to become thieves closely resemble the methods of motivating people to become doctors, businessmen, lawyers or carpenters. And, to carry the logic of the argument through, society is so structured to motivate people to occupy these various positions because the positions themselves are useful for society—the thief no less than the professor. The importance of the professional thief to "society"—at least to those who benefit most from the constituted order—makes it clear why someone with Harry's talent, sensitivity and life chances would be attracted to the career he chose.

Bill Chambliss